In
in the

MW01110013

Innovative Leadership in the Nonprofit Organization: Strategies for Change

Miriam P. Kluger
and
William A. Baker

Child Welfare League of America
Washington, DC

Child Welfare League of America, Inc.
440 First Street, NW, Suite 310, Washington, DC 20001-2085

Current Printing (last digit)
10 9 8 7 6 5 4 3 2 1

Cover and text design by Paul H Butler
Printed in the United States of America

ISBN # 0-87868-567-7

C ontents

Acknowledgments

This book is drawn from our experiences at the Village for Families and Children. We would like to thank the special people who were on the agency's leadership team during the development of these tools: Ethel Fried, Howard Garval, Abdul-Rahmaan Muhammad, Anne Pidano, and Sue Wert. Their suggestions and direct involvement made the development of these models possible.

We would also like to thank the agency's board of directors for their receptiveness to change and new ideas. James H. Vineburg commissioned and appointed the strategic planning task force and focused on the need for board improvement. James C. Ervin, Jr. provided leadership during the development and implementation of the strategic plan.

The agency staff spent many hours providing information, responses, and suggestions during the development of these models. The authors are especially grateful to research associates Kristine Mika, Patricia Mace, and Eleanor Lyon for their help not only in developing some of these models, but also in collecting and analyzing data.

We would also like to thank our secretaries, Janice Woodberry and Teresa Colaninno, for their assistance in preparing this manuscript.

We are most grateful to our editor, Carl Schoenberg, who thoroughly and thoughtfully suggested changes to make this material as clear as possible.

And finally, we would like to thank the source of our inspiration, our families: Martin, Daniel, Hannah, and Jocelyn Kluger; and Linda, Barbara, Lisa, and Amy Baker.

Introduction

This book outlines strategies for managing change in nonprofit organizations drawn from the authors' experiences in a large New England community agency that serves children and families. It is hoped that readers will find them useful in their nonprofit organizations. They are strategies for change necessitated by shifting social, economic, political, and technological forces influencing the mission, direction, and financial viability of community service organizations.

Change has always marked the development and delivery of social welfare services in America. The technologies that exist today are as different from early efforts to respond to social welfare needs as space travel is from the horse and buggy. The most earnest yearnings for insulation from the rigors of market forces—special exemptions for nonprofit organizations—are to no avail in the 1990s. As in any organization, the future rests on the organization's ability to change as the operational climate changes.

History is the inevitable definer of contexts. Without question, the history of social welfare in America set the context for change in the authors' agency, and had to be incorporated into the development of change strategies. This introduction sets forth briefly the historical influences the authors' planning had to incorporate, influences that are likely to apply to other nonprofit organizations across the country.

Historical Perspective

Laypeople and professional human service personnel perceive the nonprofit organization as different from other organizational entities. This perception is true to a certain extent, but why it is true is not generally understood. Over the years, society has idealized the work of charity. In the early days, this work was carried out largely by volunteers who labored solely out of love and commitment. In time, the demands of charity work required the consistent presence of paid staff members to support the mission and efforts of volunteers. Those who volunteered and those who elected to make service their lifetime career were both revered in their communities and by society at large, which expected from these caring and dedicated individuals an extraordinary capacity for sacrifice in behalf of others in need. These women and men won community respect on the basis and extent of their commitment.

In addition to direct service roles, volunteers served the governing boards of charity organizations without pay. So highly did society regard this charitable endeavor that the government established special protections from taxation to promote and encourage private charitable initiatives to benefit those who were unable to care for themselves. These organizational entities were formed, and by law, are driven, by their mission. To this day, that is what separates them from commercial endeavors.

A special mystique grew up around these nonprofit organizations, and any criticism generated protective—perhaps protectionist— responses. This value-driven view of nonprofit endeavors and the institutions that carried them out encountered a certain dynamic tension as the delivery of human services became professionalized. In the early part of the twentieth century in America, it seemed to follow that if those who served with good and caring motivation and special sensitivity and intuition could help, then these same good Samaritans would be even more effective as helping agents with further education and training. With the expansion of knowledge about human development and the functioning of the mind, however, new professions emerged. Psychiatry, psychology, and social work became the sciences of community and individual rehabilitation. Concurrently, the need for stronger intervention strategies was made clear by a growing understanding that children and adults with social, emotional, and mental health impairments could be helped to achieve higher levels of functioning.

Thus came about the needed professionalization of human service providers. The new professionals of the 1930s and 1940s assumed central responsibility for the course of intervention with patients and clients, and in time, appropriately expected stronger financial recognition of their education and skills—their professional contribution to those in need. The organizations that had been the centers of charitable endeavor, the domain of volunteers, changed forever.

The growth of the helping professions and the increasing demands of communities led to a concurrent professionalization of the management of nonprofit organizations. The community support needed to meet the costs of service could no longer be won merely by articulating the importance of the service mission. Information and accountability were the linchpins of effective community organizations.

In the same period of changes in the service-providing agencies, changes no less dramatic occurred in the instruments for the encouragement of charitable giving. United Ways and other federated associations materially strengthened the ability of communities to care for those in need. Moreover, government assumed an expanding role in providing for an ever-increasing segment of society that could not achieve individual or family self-sufficiency.

The entry of government and the subsequent increase in revenues available to human services enabled the continuation of the charitable mystique that nonprofit work was exempt from the rigors of the economy and competition. In addition, the availability of government revenue resulted in the entry of proprietary for-profit entities into the delivery of human services. No longer was community caring the sole possession of the charitable nonprofit organization.

The 1980s changed all that. The federal government systematically withdrew from human services it had supported—indeed had spawned—and transferred responsibility to the states. As the 1980s closed and the economy worsened, states were forced to initiate expense reductions in the human service areas. What has followed is intense competition among nonprofit service providers, as well as with for-profit service providers, for scarce dollars. This level of competition is greatly changing the face and character of nonprofit organizations.

Changing roles within nonprofit organizations also deserve comment. From the 1950s through the 1960s, a sense of partnership existed between voluntary boards of directors and employees. The writing of this period is full of references to volunteers and staff members. Little mention is made of management. To a large degree, executive directors, who had previously been referred to as executive secretaries, were perceived as filling the role of coordinator between emerging professional staffs and volunteer board members. The title *executive director* expanded demands for executive decision-making and for increasingly sophisticated management. Yet the recognition of top management's role came slowly. It was as though such recognition would undermine the mystique that surrounded nonprofit organizations.

The nature of governance in nonprofit organizations also underwent significant change in the 1970s and 1980s. The orientation of board members changed from one grounded in a personal connection with the delivery of services to a bottom-line, information-based orientation. Many board members no longer had time to devote to extensive management activities. Titles like executive director were changed to *president* and *chief executive officer* to reflect growing expectations for executive authority and decision-making. Policy, planning, evaluation, financing, and stewardship of assets became the main concerns of nonprofit boards.

Today's Nonprofit Organization

Losses have clearly been incurred in this course of change. That heady sense of mission, of partnership, of charitable commitment, of high significance, has been assaulted. Daily transactions are more businesslike, planning more strategic, and accountability more urgent. In the long term, all these qualities are necessary for the survival of effective nonprofit human service organizations, but these changes have not been universally revered. They have stimulated some of the nastiest organizational power struggles that some communities have ever seen. Human service professionals, nonprofit volunteers, and nonprofit managers are often ill equipped to deal with the level of conflict and challenge that are inherent in this kind of change.

It goes without saying that blemishes are appearing on that special entity, the nonprofit organization. The mystique is fading fast. The nonprofit organizations that will survive into the twenty-first century will be those that can thrive on competition, effectively read community needs and priorities, deliver the right services at the right price, and be able to document their effectiveness.

The surviving nonprofit organizations will also be those that can preserve mission as the driving force for their existence and at the same time be entrepreneurial in orientation, policy development, and management. The entrepreneurial spirit is not incongruent with the charitable mission of commitment to those least advantaged in the community. Rather, it is an operational orientation, or organizational culture, that includes fostering the ability to be agile and willing to change direction. These qualities are crucial to future organizational viability and the preservation of quality services and products.

The Models

The models described in this book were developed at a large child and family service organization founded in 1809 in Hartford, Connecticut. The organization saw itself as a leader and innovator, and had, over the years, developed a diverse set of community services. It valued its important traditions, but management recognized the winds of change and set about a course of planning and adaptation intended to better position the agency for the future. By necessity, that planning included sophisticated and objective systems of accountability, which are described throughout the book.

The history of social welfare in America demonstrates that change is not new—what is new is the demand for continual change. These models represent the authors' experience in preparing a nonprofit organization for continual change. Although every organization has its unique culture and dynamics, organizations also have many characteristics in common. The models described in this book can be adapted to the distinctive needs of each reader's organization.

Governance and Board Development

Much is written about the governance of nonprofit organizations, with the emphasis on function and responsibility. From the authors' experience, there is little disagreement about primary board functions, but great differences in how boards assume responsibility and fulfill their functions. The effectiveness of boards varies widely because they are organisms shaped by the diverse motivations and interests of their members, which influence the operating style of each board and how it responds to internal and external conditions affecting the organization.

Boards often function year after year without critical assessment of their performance and without the periodic modification in structures and roles that changing conditions require. It is human nature to overlook the need to change and to hold on to what is familiar. It can be dangerous to the health of nonprofit organizations, however, to allow boards to remain functionally static. Boards that do not engage in periodic self-analysis will be brought to understand the necessity of change by conflict within the board or within the organization.

This chapter reviews what makes the nonprofit organization unique, problem-solving and change processes for boards, and the primary functions of boards of directors.

Unique Qualities of Nonprofit Organizations

Governance cannot succeed in a nonprofit organization without an understanding of how it differs from the for-profit organization. The main difference is in the purpose of the organization—a for-profit organization strives to make money, while a nonprofit organization aims to provide the best service it possibly can [Koteen 1989]. The nonprofit organization is also given legitimacy by its mission. A mission statement conveys two essentials about an entity: what it is and what it does [Falsey 1989]. The nonprofit organization's mission gives it governmental sanction, exemption from taxation, and legal and community legitimacy. It is commissioned to provide services that fulfill the mission, serving the interest of communities rather than the interest of its owners. There are no owners in the usual sense; the community is as close as the nonprofit organization comes to having owners.

Board members, top management, and staff members are then only the human resources necessary to forward the organization's mission of service. Although they invest a great deal of time, energy, and other resources, and although they may be strongly committed, they are not entitled to any of the organization's assets. Within the context of the mission, the board as a whole is charged with responsibility for setting organizational direction and for determining the boundaries within which top management and direct service providers operate. The board may initiate a change in the organization's mission, or vote whether or not to accept a revised mission as suggested by top management.

Nonprofit organizations are also consumers of goods and services, which can create conflicts of interest for board members and conflict in their governance. A high standard of propriety prevails for charitable organizations. Nonprofit organizations are repeatedly called upon to demonstrate the presence of policies governing conflicts of interest in licensing and accreditation processes. Board minutes are reviewed by multiple independent examiners to assure conflict-free governance. This requires that board service be in behalf of the greater community, not the board members' personal needs.

The Processes of Problem-Solving and Change

Signs of Problems with Agency Governance

A variety of signs can suggest problems with agency governance. One may be board dialogue that focuses on issues that are top management's responsibility rather than the board's responsibility. At the opposite extreme are boards that have abdicated policy development to a strong manager or to a small nucleus of board members. In such organizations, attendance at board meetings is poor and participation lifeless. Debate is notably lacking and the level of disagreement over issues is low. The needed sense of universal mission and purpose is absent.

Other signs of problems with an organization's governance are the selection of board members without purpose and board members who are unclear about what is expected of them. The organization enters a state of drift that is interrupted only by a major crisis.

Organizational crisis can also strike when the board does examine its functional performance, finds weaknesses, and takes corrective action. Here, the risk lies in provoking change that threatens to outmode common experiences and culture. One weakness may lie in the existing relationships. The relationships between board members and top management, board members and staff members, and top management and staff members, for example, may be codependent relationships, where interactions are guided by the need and will to preserve the known operating culture regardless of its effectiveness in changing times. When a passive, dependent board of directors makes a shift to a firmer, more aggressive policy development stance, for instance, it creates a disconnectedness from the culture that top management and staff members understand. The reaction of top management and other staff members may be to act in ways that create pressure to return to the known operational culture. As in codependent relationships, all too often it takes a significant event, usually a crisis, to stimulate the examination needed to begin adjustment to change.

Governance Review

Ideally, an organization would engage in the governance review process without having first experienced a crisis. In reality, it is likely that a crisis will precipitate the examination. Even post-crisis planning, however, can and should yield important changes in the organization's governance and operating culture.

The board of directors may begin the process by commissioning a task force to investigate the current governance. Does the existing written document reflect current practice? Is the document no longer appropriate given changes in the environment? Have there been signs that the governance is no longer adequate, such as a significant crisis? The answers to these questions may be explored initially by a board task force and reported back to the board at large.

Problem Identification

A retreat for all board members with the executive director is critical to the identification of problems. Those attending the retreat can brainstorm problems in the functioning of the board and its existing governance. Possible problems may include

- Role confusion among board, executive committee, and top management with regard to the organization's policy, planning, and operations;
- Dissatisfaction with the effectiveness and efficiency of board committees and the board at large;
- Excessive demands on board members' time;
- Unclear expectations for individual board member performance;
- Weakened accountability for the board, top management, and staff as a consequence of role and authority confusion;
- Communication problems among the staff, top management, and the board;
- Inability to make timely decisions, resulting in staff members, top management, and board members feeling frustrated;
- Inefficient use of the talents and expertise of board members;
- Unrealistic demands placed on top management to support the board's activities at a time when operational demands require increasing time and attention.

These problems in functioning will lead to the formation of objectives for the new governance. For example, if retreat participants felt that the time demands placed on board members were excessive, then an objective of the new governance might be reducing the frequency of board meetings. If board members reported role confusion among board, executive committee, and top management, then an objective of the new governance might be clarifying roles and responsibilities. Resulting discussion at the retreat or in smaller board task force meetings could then identify the important responsibilities of the board.

Primary Functions of Boards of Directors

The board of directors is expected to fulfill four primary functions: (1) setting policy; (2) establishing organizational goals and evaluating outcomes; (3) hiring and replacing the chief executive officer; and (4) acting as stewards of the organization's assets [Yarrow 1989]. These functions belong solely to the board of directors, and when the board acts on them through resolution and vote, the result is the promulgation of governing policy. Figure 1 outlines the responsibilities of board members. Top management and staff members assist in formulating and recommending policy, but only the board may decide governing policy.

Figure 1. Typical Responsibilities for
Nonprofit Organization Board Members

1. Setting organizational direction
   - Amending the organization's mission as required
   - Establishing long-term strategic objectives
   - Setting policy to meet strategic objectives
   - Approving annual operating budgets

2. Employing the chief executive officer
   - Establishing annual and long-term performance objectives for the executive
   - Evaluating the annual and long-term performance of the executive
   - Providing public recognition and acceptance of the executive's operational decisions

3. Approving or disapproving management's proposals in such policy areas as major capital expenditures and contracts

4. Advising the chief executive officer on operations when consultation is sought

5. Receiving and evaluating information from top management
   - Seeking and receiving regular and special reports on the organization's performance
   - Assuring compliance with laws, standards, and licenses

6. Acting as a public community resource for the organization on local, regional, and national matters affecting the organization and its mission

7. Assuring the development of financial resources
   - Setting overall investment policies and overseeing the investment of the organization's assets
   - Engaging in the development of new financial resources
   - Monitoring the fiscal position of the organization

8. Assuring the viability of the board of directors
   - Developing board membership through its nominating and member development activities
   - Selecting and preparing board officers for their new duties
   - Monitoring financial contributions of board members
   - Coaching and mentoring board members to assure their strongest involvement and commitment

 6   Innovative Leadership in the Nonprofit Organization

Board Member Selection

Selection and development of board members are central to meeting the nonprofit organization's need for board leadership. Criteria may be identified to strengthen the selection process. First and foremost, board candidates should have demonstrated an interest in the organization's mission. The organization's needs for knowledge, skills, experience, and interests must also guide the nomination of new board members. Figure 2 outlines four categories of desirable board members.

Beyond the ability to connect with mission and the skills and experience a potential board member may have, other attributes are also important to a strong board of directors. Candidates for board membership should be chosen for their leadership potential, and should also demonstrate

- capacity to understand formal organization;
- willingness and ability to give the required time and effort to the organization;
- ability to assess issues and state views;
- ability to accept and support democratically made decisions; and
- ability and willingness to represent the organization to the community.

It is essential for board members to understand what is expected of them. To promote clarity about roles, the board must not only identify the officers it believes the organization needs, but also write job descriptions for each of these positions.

Board Committees

The current board committee structure should be examined by a board task force or in a full board retreat. Are there too many committees? Are some committees ineffective? Is effort duplicated? What changes could be made to streamline and expedite decision-making? What is the most efficient and personally rewarding use of board members' and top management's time? Answers to these questions should lead to an improved committee structure, with task descriptions for each committee.

Assessment of New Governance

After the new governance has been adopted by the board and has been in place for perhaps a year, it is important to determine how well it is working. Each area of governance that was modified should be examined. The original task force that oversaw the development of the new governance might

Figure 2. Qualified Board Members

1. Those possessing particular knowledge or skills, such as
   - Financial management
   - Investments
   - Policy development in the nonprofit services field
   - Law
   - Organizational development
   - Human resources management
   - Automation and information management
   - Communications
     - Internal
     - External (public relations or advertising)
   - Influence
     - Political (federal, state, local)
     - In the business community
     - Among the users of the organization's services
2. Those with the ability and willingness to make significant financial contributions, such as
   - Individual donors
   - Representatives of donor groups
   - Corporate donors
3. Those representing key constituencies
4. Others who have significant interest in the organization

commission such a study, with information to be collected confidentially by the organization's researcher(s). Individual interviews with board members and top management, a board and top management retreat, or a mail survey are all ways in which this information can be obtained. Questions would include how satisfied each individual is with the

- overall functioning of the board;
- clarity of board members' responsibilities;
- changes in board members' responsibilities;
- way in which new board members are selected;
- structure of board committees; and
- clarity of board committees' responsibilities.

The study would identify old weaknesses that continue and new problems that resulted from revising the governance. Periodic review and revision will assure that board governance continues to be modified appropriately.

The Experience of the Village for Families and Children

This agency began its review in the late 1980s with the identification of governance problems. Following some unpopular board budget decisions, a crisis occurred at the organization, involving significant internal disruption. During this period, the board was called upon to evaluate and determine the organization's position on matters related to the crisis, which centered on the roles and authority of the board, the chief executive officer, and the management. The board commissioned a task force to investigate the crisis and report back to the full board. The task force found that the organization lacked a clear differentiation of board and management roles and authority.

The organizational and governance problem-solving began in the management of the crisis, but the emergence of differences in the expectations of individual board members resulted in an afternoon-long retreat that was divided into two sections. The first dealt with the changing roles and functions of board members across the nation, drawing on a white paper prepared by Dr. Robert Rice, then executive vice president of Family Service America, Inc. [Rice 1986].

Rice highlighted changes in the motivations and participation of board members in the 1980s as compared to earlier times. He characterized board members as either traditional or new-wave, drawing sharp distinctions between the traditional board member—who emphasizes connection with the mission, personal values, and the direct delivery of services—and the new-wave board member—who is inclined to focus on numbers, the bottom line, and verifiable outcomes. He found that boards were generally a mixture of the two orientations. This ensured a dynamic tension in nonprofit organizational boards across the country. Rice's presentation helped members of the agency's board of directors place their own sense of conflict into perspective and view the tensions they felt as normal for boards in the late 1980s.

The second area of retreat inquiry was the identification of problems in the agency's current board governance, including the way in which the board conducted its business. A brainstorming process identified nine problems, many of which have been described earlier in this chapter. This roster of functional problems led to the formation of objectives for the governance planning process that followed. Changes in governance, for example, would have to clarify roles and responsibilities, improve board and committee efficiency, and make better use of board members' talents and expertise.

During many months of meetings, a board task force examined each of the nine problems and developed possible solutions. This work positioned the board to address one of its objectives: that board members understand what is expected of them. To further promote clarity about roles and expectations, the task force identified the officers it believed the agency needed and wrote job descriptions for each officer. These descriptions are set forth in Appendix A.

Having specified what skills and experiences the organization needed from board members, and what work the board ought to focus on, task force members realized that a very large board was not necessary. The bylaws had previously been amended to provide for up to 40 board members. This change was based on the agency's assumption of programs and board members from a local organization that had terminated services after 90 years. The task force concluded that a board this large did not improve the quality of decisions, but rather, unduly increased the management burden.

Consistent with the search for clear expectations, the board's committee structure was streamlined to more efficiently use board members' and top management's time. Constructive involvement of board members would be best achieved, it was decided, through active and focused committee work. To guide the development of board committees, job descriptions were prepared for each committee, as shown in Appendix B.

Communication was a critical component of planning and change. During the course of planning, great care was taken to communicate progress at every board and executive committee meeting. A document was prepared that sought to anticipate questions and provide answers before voting on adoption of the new governance. (See Appendix C.) The board approved the recommended changes to agency governance, and the agency's counsel then amended the organization's bylaws accordingly.

The board's strategic planning and evaluation committee recently commissioned an evaluation of the new governance. In general, board members and top management are satisfied with the changes.

Inevitably, however, several new problems were encountered. To cite one example: Perhaps as a consequence of attending fewer meetings, board members felt they did not have a clear understanding of the work of the agency. The committee therefore developed a plan for continuing education that includes activities to bring board members greater understanding of, and connectedness to, the agency.

The present governance will continue to be examined periodically in a planful, rather than a crisis-driven mode.

References

Falsey, T. A. (1989). *Corporate philosophies and mission statements: A survey and guide for corporate communicators and management.* New York: Quorum.

Koteen, J. (1989). *Strategic management in public and nonprofit organizations.* New York: Praeger.

Rice, R. M. (1986). *Report from the Field.* Available from Family Service America, 11700 West Lake Park Drive, Milwaukee, WI 53224.

Yarrow, J. H. (1989). *Corporate responsibilities of a board of directors.* (Available from the Institute for Nonprofit Training and Development, Inc., 275 Windsor Street, Hartford, CT 06120-2991.)

2

Developing the Leadership Team

Responsibilities of the Team

The ever-present function of any top management team is to provide leadership that enables the organization to realize its philosophy, mission, strategy, and annual objectives and goals. Major operational and procedural policies must be developed and carried out. The top management or leadership team must also make certain that the flow of funds permits the organization to make steady progress toward the achievement of its mission, and that funds are allocated properly to reflect present needs and future potential.

The team must maintain an organizational climate that attracts, retains, and motivates top-quality people—both professionals and volunteers. The team must also represent the organization in public forums and develop and maintain the community networks that are crucial to the operation, functioning, and development of the organization's services.

To be effective, the leadership group must develop and maintain a sense of teamwork. Candor during discussion is encouraged, as is unified support once a decision has been reached. Good teamwork can exist only when the leadership team has a unified vision of how the organization should be managed, and what organizational character and culture are desirable. Team members, however, should feel free to contribute individual ideas based on their experience, professional orientation, and personal philosophy.

11

Selecting the Team

An effective leadership team must (1) accomplish its goals; (2) sustain itself internally; and (3) develop and adjust in ways that enhance its effectiveness [Johnson and Johnson 1975]. Further, Johnson and Johnson comment that group members should have the skills to remove roadblocks to the fulfillment of group goals, to rectify problems in sustaining high-quality interactions among team members, and to conquer obstacles to becoming a more effective team.

Commissioning and Shaping the Team

The team may consist of individuals responsible for service areas, administrative services, research, communication and development, and finances. Those developing the team must claim a purpose for the team they are organizing. If the group's purpose is not understood or accepted, members may be more concerned about personal benefits from membership than they are about the destiny of the team [Zander 1985].

Regardless of title, members of the leadership team should feel free to participate equally in discussion and decision-making. This kind of participation will foster involvement and satisfaction among group members, and fully utilize the special skills, talents, and resources of each team member [Johnson and Johnson 1975]. One potential problem is the team member who has a history of negative experiences with previous leadership teams, and therefore comes to the group with preconceived pessimistic notions. Any such difficulties should be discussed openly with the full team. The lessons that can be learned from previous negative experiences should be applied to the current situation.

Selection of team members by the chief executive may be consciously or subconsciously based on achieving a balance of styles, skills, and experiences. It is important to have variability in problem-solving styles and tolerance for risk-taking and ambiguity, as well as a compatibility among all the members that enables them to work well with the top executive and with one another. Good communication skills and cultural diversity are also essential to the quality of a leadership team. While convictions and ethics should not be compromised, the ability to give and take and to negotiate is an important attribute. In addition to particular qualities that would complement strengths and meet team needs, individual members must also meet job requirements for their area of responsibility outside of the leadership team.

Once the team has been established, its objectives should be reiterated and/or clarified. Objectives might include

- effective planning and problem-solving;
- effective communication and support among team members;
- effective use of the diverse skills, experience, and ideas of the team;
- a common leadership view of organizational direction, effectiveness, and needs; and
- a central leadership forum that broadens knowledge of the organization's diverse activities, issues, problems, and problem-solving strategies.

Decision-making is a key responsibility for top management, so it is important to formalize its role in the process. The multiple levels of responsibility defy a clear, specific definition of decision-making for the leadership team, however, as the examples that follow make clear.

- A service element like a new client fee schedule must be developed by those who administer it, yet the leadership team should know about the issues, decisions, and implementation plans.
- Operational elements, such as microautomation, should be developed by the group most familiar with each element, yet the leadership group needs to know about the issues, decisions, and implementation plans.
- Personnel policies are decided by the board of directors, but must also involve full and complete input from the leadership team.
- The leadership team must identify and prioritize key problems—such as needed human resources policies, financial issues, and client-related protocols—that have to be put into the total work context.
- Some issues, particularly those that would affect the whole organization, can be decided by consensus or vote of the leadership team.
- Each member of the team brings a point of view and specific experience, skills, and attributes. It is not necessary to be in a particular position, such as that of human resources director, to offer valuable ideas. The team must understand that it is responsible not for telling team members how they should do their jobs or what decisions they should make, but rather for strengthening the input and information available to each member in her or his individual role.

In short, the leadership team must decide where final decision-making authority rests on a case by case basis. The leadership team's role in decision-making can grow if the team makes the necessary investment. The potential for this growth will be directly affected by how each team member approaches his or her team role. An openly supportive, noncompetitive arena will enable the team to develop rapidly toward this way of functioning.

Developing Management's Vision for the Organization

Changes in funding patterns and community needs often create a dynamic tension between the nonprofit organization's traditional values and community interests. As the innovative organization continues to evolve and pursue new kinds of services, clear statements about how new endeavors fit with one another and with the organization as a whole may be missing. One of the team's key jobs is the development of a management vision that encompasses recent and future changes. This vision will steer the organization into the future as it defines and clarifies the organization's current purpose, or mission. Essentially, the vision, as eloquently defined by Hickman and Silva [1984], is

1. A mental journey from the known (present) to the unknown (future), creating the future from a montage of current facts, hopes, values, possibilities, opportunities, and barriers;
2. The determinant of success or failure; and
3. The union of the strategy and culture of the organization.

The role of a visionary leader, then, is to take the organization where it has not been before. Visionary leadership creates the vision and establishes its goals. It also creates oneness among team members, because it is necessarily worked on together. The final product represents development of a course of action that is fully owned by the team. This sense of ownership is particularly important when individual team members labor daily in different and narrower arenas outside of their role on the leadership team.

In developing a vision, the leadership team should consider what it wants the organization to be doing and known for three to five years from now. It is the board's responsibility to set strategic direction, but it is the responsibility of key management to translate that into practice. The seven steps that follow may be used to develop a vision for the nonprofit organization.

Step 1. Develop a Compelling Vision of the Organization
Team members may approach this task by individually completing
sentences such as, "Three years from now, our organization will

Do...
Have...
Serve...
Be known as...
Have a reputation for..." [Plambeck 1988].

Responses may then be shared, and consensus reached. Alternatively, the group may brainstorm together to develop a vision.
Whether the initial approach is as individuals or as a group, consensus is important to build a sense of teamwork and give direction to
the organization.

One example of a vision statement for a nonprofit organization is
the following, developed at the authors' Hartford, Connecticut, agency:

The agency exists to support and strengthen families throughout
the Capital Region of Connecticut.

To achieve this vision, the agency will be

- Responsive to changing community needs;
- Sensitive to the special needs of diverse markets and con-
  sumers;
- Notable for the excellence of its services;
- Innovative and flexible in its selection of service strategies;
- Anticipatory in its understanding of, and response to,
  changing family needs;
- Committed to families and family members at risk;
- Involved in the amelioration of community problems that
  impair family functioning; and
- Engaged in the prevention of family and family member
  breakdown.

Step 2. Develop a Common Vision for Management
In this next step, the keys to realizing the vision have to be identified.
Using a one-to-two-day retreat format, the team might brainstorm
about how it would like to be known to the rest of the organization.
For example, does the team want to be known for risk-taking and
timely decision-making? Does it want to have a reputation for being
readily available to staff members and acknowledging staff members
for jobs well done?

The process of developing a vision for management is as important as its actual content. Because team members have developed it
together, the team is able to own it as a group. What follows is an
excerpt from the management vision developed by the leadership
team at the authors' organization.

The agency's management vision will include

- A commitment to change as a matter of process rather
  than as an event;
- A commitment to the belief that a culturally diverse work-
  force is crucial to effective community service;
- Proactive planning, and strategic use of financial and physical resources;
- A dedication to the principle that timely decision-making
  and risk-taking are crucial to vibrant corporate health; and
- Use of the agency's research capability as an instrument for
  enhancing agency and professional identity in the community.

In most instances, organizations reflect the vision, or lack of it, of
the top leadership. At the authors' organization, for example, the top
executive held a vision for leadership in the agency that was
expressed in the name he gave the key staff who reported to him, and
who carried responsibility for operational management throughout
the organization. He wanted group members to see themselves and
their group as leaders, rather than as managers attending to tasks. He
wanted the members of the group to influence, guide direction, and
change the course. He rejected names like "the Cabinet" or "the Management Team," electing instead to call the group "the Leadership
Forum." He wanted its members to take on characteristics of leadership, that is, to help develop and be identified with a vision for the
future. He wanted the key people to be more than managers who "do
things right"; he wanted them to be leaders who "do the right things."
[Bennis and Nanus 1985].

The top executive also believed that changing the agency's leadership culture was crucial to meeting the challenges of diminished
human service funding and intensified competition from both the nonprofit and for-profit communities. This orientation led to the processes
for developing the leadership team that are outlined in this chapter.

Step 3. Convert the Vision to Goals and Establish Priorities
Once the vision has been developed, the goals, or what must take
place to fulfill the vision, have to be identified. The goals should

incorporate both the organizational and management visions. Some of the goals developed at the authors' agency were

- Agency management and leadership shall be future-oriented, anticipatory, and proactive;
- The agency shall be known as the most experienced, qualified, able, and responsive resource for families in the Capital Region; and
- The access of clients to the agency's services shall be improved.

Once the goals have been identified, they should be rank-ordered from highest to lowest priority. Not everything can be done at once, and it is important to put the most critical and important goals first.

Step 4. Create Strategic Objectives with Measurable Expectations
In this step, the team further specifies the goal statements in measurable terms. If they are not conveyed in such terms, progress cannot be assessed objectively. This statement may represent a shift in thinking that is unfamiliar or uncomfortable for some nonprofit organizations.

To improve the access of clients to the agency's services (the third of the goals noted above), three strategic objectives were specified.

1. Centralize client intake to provide
   - Initial telephone contact within the day;
   - In emergencies, contact with the clinician within 12 hours;
   - In nonemergency cases, first appointment within one week of initial contact;
   - Waiting period for service beyond the initial visit not to exceed one month;
   - Cultural diversity in the Intake Unit consistent with the cultural identifications of consumers; and
   - Coordination between central and satellite offices.

2. Improve accessibility for consumers by reducing employee turnover in the following ways
   - Maintain availability of up to 35 hours of professional training per year;
   - Control distribution of multiproblem, crisis cases to 80% of the cases assigned to any clinician;
   - Give each clinician at least one case in another service or unit of the agency;

- Require one professional service innovation per year;
- Offer clinicians the opportunity to enhance their earning ability by providing up to six hours of supplemental pay for direct service per week; and
- Fulfill the annual competitive pay objectives.

3. Improve access to the agency's services on the part of minority consumers by
   - Creating and implementing a long-term program to recruit minority professionals (for example, through encouraging high school students to enter the human services field), and
   - Investing in a recruitment effort sufficient to ensure at least one available minority candidate for every job opening.

Step 5. Charter a Sound Planning Process

To fulfill the strategic objectives, new guidelines should spell out what the planning would cover, within what time frames, and within what necessary budgetary and other restrictions or constraints.

For example, the following elements were worked out at the authors' agency in developing a centralized intake service

- A location and facilities plan
- Staffing requirements
- Hours of operation
- Supervisory authority
- Job descriptions that identify roles, responsibilities, and authority
- A training plan
- Linkage of centralized intake to other agency computerized information systems
- Revision of forms
- Information and referral capability and policies
- A communications plan for referral sources
- A definition of *emergency*
- A strategy for handling emergencies
- Agreements with agency service units, including procedures for assigning intake cases
- Management of involuntary clients
- Impact on accounting and clerical staff
- A budget plan

- A plan for inclusion of other business functions (such as fee setting, agency procedures, nonpayment procedures)
- Identification of planning responsibility and expected date for completing the plan
- Implementation timetable that achieves objectives by ____.

Step 6. Assign Responsibilities

At this point, strategic objectives are assigned to leadership team members. An objective may be the sole responsibility of one team member or it may be assigned to more than one person. Assigning more than one person to an objective stimulates collaborative teamwork. The downside, however, is the possibility of uneven distribution of the workload and potential resentment among team members.

The experiences, strengths, and interests of individual team members play a role in assigning the objectives. Other factors are work styles and relative comfort with working under the pressure of short deadlines, or networking and coordinating with other staff members. Ideally, the distribution of assignments is a group activity. The balance between individual workloads and the priority assigned to each objective plays a role in determining who will be responsible for the objective. In extreme cases, some team members may have many objectives assigned to them while others have none—or the number of objectives assigned to each team member could be the same, but because of the relative priority of individual objectives, many of those assigned to one team member could have very immediate deadlines with no possibility of on-time completion. The team member's interest, rather than equity of workload, however, may be the predominant factor in successful accomplishment of assigned responsibilities.

Step 7. Monitor Fulfillment of the Plan

The vision statement and its accompanying objectives provide a basis for assessing team performance. Although the vision was developed with the assistance of the full leadership team, the supporting objectives are assigned to individuals, or perhaps pairs of team members. A handy tool for outlining activities and timelines associated with each objective is the Gantt Chart [Gantt 1961]. Activities are listed down the left-hand side of the matrix, in sequential order, and units of time—typically weeks or months—needed to complete each activity are listed in columns across the top.

Monitoring by team members should be periodic—at least quarterly. Its purpose is not only to assess progress, but also to provide a resource to team members who might like assistance in problem-solving or in reviewing ideas or next steps. Folded into individual objectives are strategic priorities and other responsibilities as outlined in personal job descriptions. When workloads are heavy and day-to-day responsibilities crowd schedules, the monitoring also helps keep the vision at the forefront, acting as a reminder to the leadership team.

The realization of an organization's vision is only as good as its monitoring. If no mechanism is in place to monitor progress in accomplishing the objectives of the vision, it is hard to imagine that the organization's leadership is truly committed to its achievement. It may be easy to overlook this last step after all the hard work that has gone on up to this point, but it is the critical step that moves the vision from rhetoric to reality.

At the authors' agency, the very nature of the vision, which included timely decision-making, also reinforced the importance of monitoring. Further, viewing change as a process rather than as a special event lends itself to continual monitoring as changes unfold. At this agency, monitoring occurred quarterly as part of leadership team meetings as well as individually with the top executive on an as-needed basis. Strategic objectives were laid out on Gantt charts, and the charts were reviewed line by line. Plans might be altered during these meetings, and an explanation of the amendment given. Team members were available as a resource to other team members to discuss any issues that arose between quarterly reports to the full leadership team.

Evaluating the Team's Planning and Performance

The leadership group's planning and performance as a team must also be evaluated. Typically, the leadership team will meet weekly or every other week. This not inconsequential amount of time should be used as productively as possible. One team member may be given the task of collecting performance information, such as

- Did the meeting start and end on time?
- Were agendas, minutes, and other necessary materials distributed in advance of meetings?
- Were no more than two major items on the agenda?
- What percentage of agenda items were completed?

- Was time available for
  - urgent issues?
  - human resource matters?
  - announcements?
  - determination of new agenda items?
  - communications to the staff?
  - schedule planning?
  - preparing the agenda for the next leadership team meeting?

Knowing that meetings are being monitored in itself improves the effectiveness of meetings. Quarterly reports are made on how well the team as a whole is doing. How issues that arise during meetings are managed is also monitored. For example, a team member may raise a new consideration in conjunction with an agenda item under discussion. The monitor will record the issue, the date it was discussed, whether a deadline for returning to it was assigned, the date of that deadline, and whether the deadline was met. The monitor may also track task assignments that are given during the team meeting. A description of the task, the name of the team member it was assigned to, and the date it was assigned may all be recorded and referred back to periodically, or whenever confusion arises about who received the assignment. Sharing of information from the literature on meeting effectiveness and team performance may accompany these quarterly reports.

Managing the Bumps

Despite a careful selection of team members and a unified vision, there will be times when progress does not flow as smoothly as anticipated. One bump in the road may concern the clarification of roles and responsibilities. Although a large portion of the team's work may occur with all group members present, responsibilities or particular tasks will be delegated to individuals. Any area of confusion, such as who will develop a client fee-set policy or who will review and select the employee health insurance package, has to be cleared up, and disagreements reconciled.

Bumps may also develop during the budgeting process. Territoriality problems may arise despite previous feelings of solid team cohesiveness, but this may sometimes be viewed favorably as a demonstration of strong commitment. Budgeting as related to downsizing may be personalized: one service or division may feel pitted against another, and client services and administrative supports may seem to be in conflict. Although it is important to emphasize the overarching needs of the organization rather than its individual parts, these conflicts should be openly raised, openly acknowledged when they appear, and openly discussed.

The top executive should set the tone for the group as well as the rest of the organization. He or she should take as much time as necessary to achieve consensus. The executive also should be willing to make explicit orally what he or she believes, rather than communicate nonverbally. The executive must assume seldom and explain frequently. There is no room for "The leadership team members know what I mean, and I know what he or she thinks."

People have personal characteristics that inevitably create tension points, but these points of conflict can and should be viewed as natural. Interpersonal bumps between team members will arise on occasion. A lack of communication or a misunderstanding may play a role in these incidents, and should be examined carefully. In dealing with conflicts, the first step is for the parties to resolve their differences privately, promptly, and honestly. They owe the leadership team this effort. Only when this fails should the disagreement be escalated to a meeting with the executive director, or, if appropriate (or if team members are affected), with the entire leadership team.

Trust and Oversight

One leadership team member may have the responsibility for monitoring the accomplishment of objectives derived from the vision; another member may monitor the effectiveness of team meetings. For these assignments to be a possibility or even have credibility, the team members must trust one another. At the authors' organization, for example, the chair of the weekly leadership team meetings rotates among the members. Each chair in turn is responsible for preparing the agenda and running the meeting. This approach demonstrates the executive director's trust in the team and willingness to share this responsibility.

Team members' different styles in approaching problem-solving can be useful only if trust is present. The team as a whole must be able to feel, without judgment, that the styles of individual members allow each to contribute uniquely to the effectiveness of the team. Trust develops over time, but if the team has had a good start, trust will gradually unfold. In this, as in other ways, the development of the team does not have a beginning or an end. Teamwork continues to evolve as long as the team exists.

References

Bennis, W. and Nanus, B. (1985). *Leaders: The strategies for taking charge.* New York: Harper & Row.

Gantt, H. (1961). *Gantt on Management.* New York: American Management Association.

Hickman, C. A., & Silva, M. A. (1984). *Creating Excellence.* New York: Plume Publishing.

Johnson, D. A., and Johnson, F. P. (1975). *Joining together—Group theory and group skills.* Englewood Cliffs, NJ: Prentice-Hall.

Plambeck, D. L. (March 1988). "Developing Organizational Integrity." Presentation at the United Way of America conference, Hartford, CT.

Zander, A. (1985). *The purposes of groups and organizations.* San Francisco: Jossey-Bass.

3

Setting the Organization's Direction: Strategic Planning

In the face of changing funding climates, new social trends, and population shifts, nonprofit organizations must be aggressive and innovative to retain their ability to serve the needs of the community. Strategic planning, originally applied in the corporate arena, has become increasingly popular in the nonprofit sector. Coming from a combination of the Greek words for army (stratos) and leader (ego), strategy defines an organization's purpose and direction. The strategic planning process encourages decision-making based in part on an assessment of the current environment and what this means to the future of the organization. It also encourages risk-taking, organized efforts, systematic feedback, and a frank examination of the organization as it currently is, including its strengths and weaknesses.

First, strategic planning offers a framework for helping an organization anticipate growing needs and preparing it to meet rising demands in an organized, reasonable fashion based on careful internal and external feasibility analyses. Strategic planning operates by developing a picture or vision of the ideal organization and then determining what must be done to get there. Planners consider a host of possible futures and their implications for current decisions and actions. They keep options open in case the future does not turn out as anticipated.

Second, strategic planning helps the organization set or define its priorities. A multitude of needs strains the resources of many nonprofits, yet an organization can't do everything at once. Which issues, problems, or needs are most important and should be addressed first?

25

Third, strategic planning can help the nonprofit organization to develop a coherent and defensible basis (or strategy) for decision-making. Decisions are purposeful, not haphazard. The policies and actions that flow from strategic planning largely define the organization's services.

Fourth, strategic planning is action-oriented, and helps top management personnel to do their jobs within a dynamic, changing setting. A plan of action often contains qualitative rather than quantitative changes; for example, instead of deciding to do more of something old, the organization may introduce a new service.

Fifth, strategic planning requires the participation of all staff members. Teamwork is essential. Nurturing commitment to and ownership of the plan encourages staff members to support, rather than feel threatened by, organizational change.

Sometimes strategic planning is confused with long-range planning, but there are significant differences. Whereas long-range planning first specifies goals and objectives and then translates them into current budgets and work programs, strategic planning stresses identifying and resolving issues. It also emphasizes assessing the internal and external environment, rather than extrapolating current trends into the future. This tendency often leads an organization to consider only one possible path, which may be harmful if the future does not turn out as anticipated. This limiting of options is also likely to result in quantitative shifts, rather than the qualitative shifts that take place when an organization is guided by a strategic plan with a vision of success.

To summarize, strategic planning is an important ingredient for survival, especially in turbulent times. By anticipating future needs and breaking out of traditional molds to make qualitative rather than quantitative changes—changes based on a vision of the ideal—nonprofit organizations can deal with the critical challenges inherent in today's dynamic environment.

Key Components of Strategic Planning

There are several different approaches to strategic planning. Because planning must be tailored to the specific situation, nearly every planning process, in practice, will be a hybrid of these approaches [see Bryson 1988, Drucker 1973, and Henderson 1979].

What are the major components of strategic planning? To a greater or lesser degree, every strategic plan should include, as elaborated below, (1) a situational or internal environmental assessment; (2) an external environmental assessment or scan; (3) identification of strategic priorities; (4) strategy development, including a multiyear action plan; and (5) monitoring of implementation and any revisions that may be made.

1. Situational Assessment

A situational assessment is a taking stock of the nonprofit as it is now. It is a thorough and frank internal examination of the organization's services, strengths and weaknesses, current populations served, and funding sources. These data contribute the first half of an analysis that is a primary component of the Harvard Policy Model of strategic planning [see Barry 1986]. Termed SWOT—standing for Strengths, Weaknesses, Opportunities, and Threats—the model systematically assesses the internal strengths and weaknesses of an organization in relation to the external opportunities and threats in the environment. This examination points the way to the best fit between the organization and its environment, and the strategy that flows from it.

Because each organization is unique, no one set of questions may be applied universally in a situational assessment. There are, however, several areas to consider. The first component is current resources or inputs—information on the number of staff members and their credentials, salaries, required equipment or supplies, and physical plant.

Strategy, or process, is the second component. Begin by gathering a service description and information on missions, goals, and any strategy changes within the past five years. Constraints or obstacles to service delivery and collaboration and integration within the organization are other areas to assess.

Performance, or output, is the third area to examine—how well the organization, individual service, or unit is doing its job, as measured by objective indications of quality and success. Service strengths and weaknesses should be evaluated from both the client's and the employee's perspective. The results, coupled with a comparison with the competition, are important aspects of the situational assessment. See chapter 4 for a review of outcome effectiveness studies.

Situational Self-Assessment Survey

Depending on the organization, and particularly its size, the situational assessment may be conducted in several ways. Because the authors are part of a fairly large nonprofit agency with 23 different services, the model they developed and describe here uses a situational self-assessment survey. Small organizations or single-service organizations may be able to conduct this assessment less elaborately, perhaps in a structured group meeting where discussion focuses on answering particular questions about agency services. The small organization may, however, still need the documentation that would result from the methodology about to be described—for example, when presenting its strategic plan.

Instead of imposing an evaluation made by an external source, the situational self-assessment survey engages the service providers in developing an instrument that asks the questions they think are important. If staff members are drawn into the strategic planning process, they cannot later complain that the instrument asked the wrong questions.

Soliciting survey items involves prompting staff members with questions like the following

- What questions would you ask to describe your service? Your staff members?
- What questions would you ask to find out about your program's client population? Funding? Costs?
- What questions would you ask to determine your program's strengths? Weaknesses?
- What would you like to know about your program and its functioning in the organization or the community?

A large number of questions may be generated in this way. If staff members are having difficulty coming up with ideas, a research staff member may facilitate the process by attending staff meetings, giving further examples of potential questions, and offering encouragement and reassurance.

The resulting questions are grouped by categories, such as client-related, funding-related, or service-related. Another approach groups inputs with current resources, present strategy with process, and performance with outputs.

The frequency with which each question is mentioned should be noted next to the question on a comprehensive list of all the questions generated. To determine what should be included in the final situational self-assessment survey, the compiled questions may be reviewed either by a planning group, which includes staff members from service, research, and/or administrative areas; by top management; or by some other designated team of staff members with interest, experience, and expertise in strategic planning. The desire to gather as much information as possible must be balanced with the need for an instrument that can be completed in a reasonable amount of time.

2. Environmental Scan

The community the organization serves does not remain static; new needs or challenges arise over time. By anticipating needs, and tailoring services accordingly, an agency can prepare to meet rising demands in an organized and reasonable manner.

Strategic planning encourages decision-making based in part on an examination of the present external environment and how it might affect the future of the organization. The environmental scan identifies future trends that may become opportunities or threats to the organization. This is the second part of the SWOT analysis.

The trends predicted or monitored are generally social, economic, political, or technological. Examples of social trends that may be of relevance to a nonprofit organization are demographic changes in marital status and family constellation, shifts in minority population, teen pregnancy rates, child abuse and neglect rates, rates of substance abuse and HIV/AIDS, and child care needs.

Examples of pertinent economic trends are poverty rates, the affordability and adequacy of housing, indicators for homelessness and unemployment, and competition between nonprofit and for-profit organizations. Political trends may include tax reform; national, state, and local government funding patterns; welfare reform; and access to health care. Technological trends include both advances in computer technology, including personal computers with increasingly sophisticated software, work stations, and local area networks, and biotechnology that allows the structure of genes to be changed to correct birth defects, yield new cancer treatments, and affect the course of Alzheimer's disease, stroke recovery, and the alleviation of depression.

Each of these areas will affect some organizations more than others, depending on the kind of services each one offers. National, regional, and local trends all have an impact. In conducting an environmental scan, one may encounter difficulty in placing some trends into one of the four categories. The trends often have an element of, or are a combination of, several areas, so the ultimate classification depends on personal judgment. For example, one person might consider substance abuse a social problem; another might say it is due to an economic problem, such as poverty; and a third might consider it a combination of the two. Regardless of how substance abuse trends are categorized, they are critically important to many nonprofit organizations, and should be included in an organization's environmental scan.

Sources of Information

Environmental scans are often produced by major national nonprofit organizations, such as the United Way and Family Service America. The reports are routinely sent to members or made available for a nominal fee. These scans typically provide useful information on national trends. Professional journals and national association newsletters and conferences may also be useful in understanding trends across the country.

To obtain information specific to an organization's local community or state, newspapers and local association or organization newsletters may be helpful. Other sources of information are the local chamber of commerce, local or regional polling centers, regional councils, and city or state offices of policy and management.

Critical trends currently or potentially affecting an organization may also be identified in structured focus groups with the agency's own staff members, board members, and volunteers. Other participants should include key community leaders or informants, such as public educators, researchers, public service agency administrators, legislators, local officials, judges, members of the academic community, tax experts, and competitors. The authors recommend the structured nominal group technique, or NGT.

Nominal Group Technique

Invented by Delbecq and Van de Ven [Delbecq et al. 1975], the nominal group technique, or NGT, is a method for structuring a small focus group, typically involving no more than 10 participants. It allows equal participation and equal weighting in obtaining group opinion. NGT includes individual generation of ideas on paper, round-robin recording of ideas, discussion of ideas on the master list, and voting to rank the ideas.

In this case, the facilitator would ask focus group participants to identify the most crucial trends, problems, or issues facing the community the organization serves. A confidential voting process is used to determine trend priorities for each focus group. Individual participants are asked to select the seven trends they consider most important and to number them from seven to one, with seven being the single most important trend. (Depending on the number of trends generated by the group, however, a selection of five or ten trends may be more appropriate.) The trends, problems, and issues may then be rank-ordered by votes received. (See Moore 1987 for a step-by-step, detailed description of NGT.)

After the focus groups have met, all the focus group lists are merged. This may be done by having the facilitators develop standard categories or names for the trends, eliminating items that are simply different ways of referring to the same trend. A master list of trend categories is then developed. Individual focus group lists are transferred to the generically worded categories on the master list, and votes for each trend are tallied for all participants.

The result of this effort is a rank-ordering of trends from greatest to least importance by the key stakeholders of the organization. Key stakeholders are those who are affected by, or who can influence, the future of an organization. (Examples of stakeholders in a child welfare agency might be clients, employees, and referring agencies.) Top management may choose to give equal or unequal weight to the responses of staff members, board members, volunteers, and community leaders. Further analyses, keeping the responses of staff members, board members, volunteers, and community leaders separate, are also useful in understanding the differences and similarities of these groups.

The fully ranked list may be reported, or just the top five or 10 items. This information, along with the material collected earlier from printed matter, makes up the environmental scan.

3. Strategic Priorities Identification

A planning group, which includes staff members from service, research, and/or administrative areas; top management; or some combination of the two, takes the next step toward the establishment of strategic priorities for the organization. Strategic priorities are trends, problems, or issues of critical importance to key stakeholders that the organization has chosen to address. The identification begins with information in the environmental scan—the combined master ranking of trends, problems, and issues identified by all focus group participants—which is shared with the designated planning group.

The nominal group technique is repeated after a review of information on both the social, economic, political, and technological trends, problems, or issues and the stakeholder rankings. Planning group members may be asked to select the five items from the master list that they feel are likely to best position the organization for the future. If the final list has more than 10 items, the planning group may agree to consider only the top 15, for example, at the next step in developing strategic priorities.

Internal Feasibility

It is important that the spirit of risk-taking and the vision of the ideal organization be maintained throughout the strategic planning process. Up to this point, participants have not limited their generation of trends, problems, and issues by concern about the feasibility of the organization actually implementing a related change. Before an organization can adopt a realistic set of strategic priorities, however, the internal feasibility of addressing each trend, problem, or issue on the planning group's list has to be studied. Does addressing this trend, problem or issue, for example, fit with the points in the organization's mission statement? With staff members' capabilities, skills, experience, and training? Will it mean developing new services, or expanding or enhancing existing services?

Formal documentation of the planning group's methodical review of the items is helpful. Forms may be developed to rate the top items on internal factors; relevance to the organization's mission, for example, may be rated high, medium, or low. How well would the services intended to address the trend, problem, or issue fit with staff members' current capabilities? The fit might be rated good, moderate, or poor. The result of this effort will be a grid that shows the ratings on internal factors for each of the items.

External Feasibility

To develop successful anticipatory strategies, an organization must also examine external factors. Assuming that the organization develops services in accord with a particular trend, problem, or issue, what is the level of competition? What is the growth potential for services that address this area? What potential funding or other resources are available? What is the current stage of development of these services?

External factors may be used to rate each of the top trends, problems, and issues. For example, competition or availability of others offering similar services might be rated as high, moderate, or low. The growth potential of the market—factors such as client demand—could be rated on a similar scale. Stages of development for a service typically include introduction (the client population, or market, is unaware of the service); growth (the service catches on rapidly); maturity (the market is very familiar with the service and usage is high); and decline (market interest in the service is reduced). As was done in the internal feasibility study, a summary grid can be prepared that shows the ratings of each of the top trends, problems, or issues on the relevant external factors.

The planning group then studies the information from these two grids and eliminates any of the top trends, problems, or issues that are not feasible because of internal or external factors. Following this in-depth examination and discussion, the planning group makes a final review of the remaining items, perhaps revising their rank order. Then the governing body, often a board of directors, receives this information and makes the final decision on the organization's strategic priorities.

4. Development of a Strategic Action Plan

Selected because they represent the serious trends, problems, or issues affecting the community served, the strategic priorities provide guide-lines for the expansion, enhancement, or reduction of existing services and the development of new services. Once the strategic priorities have been approved by the organization's governing body, a strategic action plan can be developed. As in previous steps, all staff members, or as many as possible, should be involved. If this is not feasible, as in a very large agency, then supervisors, middle management, and others who represent the remaining staff members should be invited to participate.

Ideally, a group of at least 10, but no more than 20 staff members brainstorms ideas for possible new services that address the strategic priorities. These ideas are grouped according to the strategic priorities that were developed. The group leader or facilitator should feel encouraged rather than alarmed if a large number of ideas are generat-ed, because the next step will subject these suggestions to internal and external feasibility studies.

Existing services, like possible new services, are also subject to inter-nal and external feasibility studies to assess their fit with the new strategic priorities. Information from the situational self-assessment survey is used in this process. Combining all information to date, ideas for new services are discussed in conjunction with changes in, or elimination of, current services that do not rate well against the feasibility factors.

In social service agencies, it is helpful at this time to identify whether the service's level of intervention addresses prevention and education prior to any difficulties; early intervention, using less than intensive services for people potentially at risk; or intensive remedia-tion for those with severe difficulties. The planning option to be used if the change is implemented—development, expansion, or enhancement—is another important piece of information. Options include a recommitment to continue current services that are relevant to the strategic priorities. Services that do not relate to the strategic priorities, and that the organization feels no need to recommit to, may be cut back or eliminated. The strategic priorities provide direction to the organization. A note of caution, however—not every service must relate to the strategic priorities. Some services that are not directly related to the strategic priorities may still be offered because they are deemed worthwhile, because they are needed, because they financially support another service, or for other valid reasons.

Services that will require intra-organizational collaboration are also identified. Top management and/or the planning group then meet several times to decide which of the new ideas proposed earlier should be strongly considered for implementation. Not all suggestions or proposals can be implemented at once. Some, upon further examination, may not rate well on internal and external feasibility factors.

Varying levels of effort may be assigned to the final priorities. Some may be considered major new efforts that will require new resources, training or recruitment of staff members, and other measures. Large new initiatives that are intra-organizational may be identified as major initiatives. Other efforts proposed may be within the context of already existing services, and will therefore require fewer resources. They will not represent as large a change, and may only affect a particular division or unit of the organization.

The list of proposed new efforts is further examined to be sure that the newly identified services are balanced. Not all can be major initiatives. Further, not all the proposed efforts should represent new services to be developed from scratch. Although the development of new services may seem the most enticing and interesting to staff members, expansion and enhancement of existing services should also be part of the organization's plans. Strategic planning results in evolutionary, rather than revolutionary, solutions. Organizational changes take place in a controlled, planful manner. A strategic plan containing only new development activities will not allow for gradual, evolutionary change that can be phased in planfully.

Descriptions of the proposed new, major intra-organizational initiatives are then prepared. These will include information on objectives, staffing and space requirements, referral sources and linkages, and timelines for proposed activities over the next three years. Each division or major unit of the organization prepares a description of the smaller efforts to occur within that unit or division. Information on the level of intervention addressed and the planning option employed are also included, as well as the one or more strategic priorities addressed. This material is presented to the organization's governing body for approval.

5. Monitoring the Plan

Once the strategic plan is approved by the organization's governing body, its progress must be formally assessed periodically. Members of the research and evaluation department or a planning group may be designated to lead the monitoring process. These individuals work with members of the board or other governing body to make sure that the resulting information will meet the board's needs. Monitoring may take place in several ways.

Overall Progress

Overall progress in addressing each of the strategic priority areas can be assessed through individual interviews or surveys developed by those responsible for evaluating progress. Top management and board members, for example, can rate general progress on each of the strategic priorities as exceeding, meeting, partly meeting, or not meeting expectations. Examples can be given in support of these ratings, and a general sense of progress determined.

Progress on Major Initiatives

Progress on each of the major initiatives can be examined separately, with the individual or group responsible for implementing the initiative formally providing a status report on efforts to date and next steps.

Progress on Additional Efforts

Through interviews or questionnaires, top management may rate progress on the proposed intradivisional efforts and include a supporting narrative. Ratings might be as follows

1. Have not yet started to address this activity

2. Are in the early planning and development stage

3. Are in an advanced stage of development and possible early implementation

4. Have implemented, accomplished, and/or completed the activity

5. Chose to abandon the activity before implementation or accomplishment

Respondents are also asked to confirm or update information on each of the additional efforts outlined in the original plan. This may include confirmation of the strategic priority addressed, planning option employed (expansion, enhancement, or new development), and level of intervention selected (prevention, intervention, or remediation).

Examples of recent training activities related to the strategic priorities should be given. A description of staff-directed community outreach activities related to the strategic priorities may be requested, if the activities are part of the strategy. A list of activities or services that had to be reduced or eliminated in order to accomplish these new efforts should be included.

A less subjective type of monitoring should also be attempted. Once the strategic priority areas have been identified and a three-year action plan developed, the agency may collect baseline data on current services as they relate to the strategic priorities. In a social service or mental health agency, for example, each client's primary problem may be related to one of the strategic priority areas or else placed in an Other category. The same data on a sample of all current cases may be collected one year later to see if a shift took place in the percentage of clients receiving treatment for problems in one of the strategic priority areas. As the strategic plan is implemented, the percentage of the agency's clients that fall into the nonstrategic priority category (Other) should decrease.

Several words of caution are in order about this monitoring technique. First, raters who are also service providers may promote their interest in showing shifts or improvements by using the Other category as little as possible. Second, as staff members become more familiar with the strategic priority categories, the definitions and inclusion/exclusion rules may be refined. Anyone who interprets the data must be aware that the way primary problems are coded may have changed over time, rather than the caseload itself. Third, the impact of staff member training or some other factor may have enhanced the service providers' ability to recognize problems stemming from one of the strategic priority areas. This training may, however, influence the type of service provided, and represent a true shift in treatment, regardless of the way in which the problem was categorized.

Selecting the appropriate problem area for a multiproblem case may be a final complicating factor. Several of the strategic priorities may go hand in hand. One underlying problem may have caused another problem, so categorization will depend on the judgment and philosophical leanings of the particular staff member.

Despite these compelling factors, monitoring is a key ingredient of successful strategic planning. Attention should be given to resolving the unique issues that arise in each organization.

The Village for Families and Children's Experience

Over the years, the Village for Families and Children has received support from a variety of sponsors. At the time of this writing, however, traditional sources of revenue are not as certain as they once were, and the problems of the clients the agency serves are growing more serious and complex. The minority population in Hartford has increased. In addition, 1990 census figures confirmed Hartford's status as the poorest city in Connecticut, with 28% of its residents living below the poverty line.

A strategic planning effort initiated in January 1988 sought a course for the agency that would take into account future trends that could affect its ability to serve clients. This comprehensive process involved all members of the staff, including top management and the board of directors, in cooperative planning. The process was inclusive in order to achieve consensus when final decisions were made. The authors began to develop a plan for future service provision that would (1) analyze and identify trends, problems, and issues in the social, economic, political, and technological arenas; (2) define and acknowledge population change; (3) assess the agency's current services; and (4) yield direction for future services that would best meet the community's needs.

Environmental Scan

An environmental scan was done, beginning with a review of available printed material concerning future trends, problems, and issues in the country, and, where available, in the Greater Hartford community. Previously published environmental scan reports from national organizations, such as the United Way and Family Service America, provided one source of information. Also useful were newspaper articles, publications from polling organizations, and reports from several national organizations, such as the National Institute of Mental Health and the National Center for Child Abuse and Neglect, and several state government organizations.

Some of the trends, problems, and issue areas researched were substance abuse, domestic violence, crime, teenage pregnancy and parenting, homelessness, AIDS, unemployment, and biotechnology. All told, the agency's environmental scan report contained descriptions of 20 social trends, seven economic trends, and nine political and technological trends.

To augment the information gleaned from printed matter, a series of focus groups was held with key stakeholders. The nominal group technique (NGT) was used, with respondents asked to identify trends, problems, and issues facing the Greater Hartford community. The focus groups each accommodated seven to 10 individuals and lasted approximately two hours. A total of 17 focus groups was held during a three-month period.

Overall, participants included 85 staff members, 17 board members, and eight agency auxiliary volunteers. Because it was also considered crucial to obtain the views of community leaders, 26 key informants from Hartford's education, welfare, and academic community participated in the focus groups.

Before the responses from the focus groups could be merged, standard categories for the trends, problems, and issues had to be developed. This was done through a group process, with six staff member evaluators reviewing the responses from each of the 17 groups. Once the master trend list was completed, votes from focus group participants were combined and tallied.

Further analyses compared the responses of staff members, board members, and community leaders. The differences and similarities among the three groups were reflected in their voting patterns, with staff members, for example, more likely to rank social problems at the top of their list, and board members, many of them from the business community, likely to rank economic problems first. This information became part of the environmental scan report, and served several purposes. In addition to providing increased understanding of the viewpoints of the various stakeholders, it demonstrated to staff members that their priorities were considered by the board of directors, the group that would ultimately set direction for the agency.

Situational Assessment

At about the same time as the environmental scan, a situational assessment was also being done, with directors and staff members evaluating the 23 agency programs. To encourage their participation and sense of ownership, staff members were given a significant role in the development of the situational assessment instrument. This process, while lengthening and complicating the task, was considered integral to obtaining pertinent information. It also helped reduce the risk of objections to the assessment tool on the part of staff members once the evaluation had been completed.

Developing the Situational Assessment Instrument

Initially, all program directors received letters encouraging their staff members to submit questions they considered meaningful for the assessment of their services. Few responded, due in part to lack of interest, hostility toward evaluations in general, and/or confusion about the request.

A notice was placed in the agency newsletter, describing the purpose of the situational assessment and giving examples of possible areas for questions. Again, there was little response or enthusiasm. Attendance at a meeting of the program directors shed some light on the problem by exposing a high degree of confusion about the task itself. Few program staff members had any experience in developing survey questions. Participants agreed that the process could be aided by having the evaluators attend individual department meetings. In these small, personal groups, more examples of question areas were given. Evaluators asked staff members: What questions would you ask to find out about

- your program's client population?
- your program's funding?
- your program's strengths?
- its weaknesses?

From seven such meetings, more than 100 questions were generated. The next task was to select questions from this large pool of items. The evaluators first developed question categories, such as service description, client description, program costs, and funding, and grouped the items accordingly. The frequency with which each questions had been mentioned in the seven groups was listed next to that item.

The agency's top management and program directors then were asked to review all the questions on the list and indicate which questions they strongly felt should be asked and which items could be excluded from the situational assessment. Development of the situational assessment survey was completed in accordance with this feedback and the frequency with which items had been mentioned. The resulting survey was a truly agencywide effort, consisting of questions generated and selected by staff members.

Establishing Strategic Priorities

After the environmental scan and the situational assessment, which took place nearly simultaneously, the strategic priorities were chosen. Then top management went through a group process that was later repeated by the board. Top management was present when board members went through the process to answer any questions and provide other needed information.

This group process consisted of a review of the environmental scan report, studying the list of 85 trends, problems, and issues identified by all the focus group participants. Which five items, if addressed, would best position the agency for the future? Each top manager confidentially selected the five items he or she considered most likely to place the Village for Families and Children in the vanguard of human service agencies in the Greater Hartford region. Then selections were merged, and all the items that had received at least one vote were rank-ordered from highest to lowest number of votes.

The top managers next discussed the trends, problems, and issues on this reduced list, highlighting their importance and implications for the agency and the Greater Hartford community now and in the next three to five years. From this list, each top manager again selected the five items most likely to place the Village for Families and Children in the vanguard of human service agencies. Selections were merged, and the items that had received at least one vote were again rank-ordered.

This latest reduced list contained 15 trends, problems, and issues. The next step was an internal feasibility study. Using forms developed for this purpose, the top managers rated each of the 15 items as high, moderate, or low in relevance to the agency's mission. They then indicated how well the services to address each trend, problem, or issue would fit the capability, skills, experience, and training of the current staff, using a rating scale of good, moderate, or poor. A third dimension was also evaluated—whether the ways to address each of these items involved creating new services or modifying existing services. This was critical to developing a balanced strategic plan that would lead to evolutionary rather than revolutionary change and build on the current strengths and expertise of the organization. After these internal factors had been considered, participants were asked to eliminate any trends, problems, or issues it no longer seemed feasible to address.

The top managers then considered several external factors in relation to this revised list. The level of competition, or availability of other organizations or individuals offering similar services, was assessed first. Assuming that the agency would develop or already had developed services related to a particular trend, problem, or issue, the top managers rated the current level of competition as high, moderate, or low. Next, the growth potential of the market in the related service area (client demand) was rated as high, moderate, or low. The supply of funding and other resources was also examined, and rated as many, moderate, or few. Finally, the current development of services related to a particular trend, problem, or issue was rated as at the stage of introduction, growth, maturity, or decline.

After this analysis of external considerations, the group eliminated any of the trends, problems, or issues that no longer seemed feasible. The trends, problems, and issues were reviewed once again, in light of all that had been discussed, with slight modifications in wording of the items and rank-ordering of the final list.

When board members repeated this process, with top management present to answer questions and provide other information, they also developed a revised list of trends, problems, and issues.

The two lists were then submitted to the strategic planning and evaluation committee of the board, a group that included the president of the agency and the staff researcher responsible for leading the strategic planning process. The lists were remarkably similar. With slight revisions, the following six strategic priorities were approved: substance abuse; domestic violence; child abuse and neglect; lack of day care; issues for divorced families, step-families, blended families, and single-parent families; and lack of parenting skills.

Developing the Strategic Action Plan

After the board approved the strategic priorities, the strategic action plan was developed. As in previous steps, as many staff members as possible were involved in this effort. Staff members reviewed the situational assessment survey in divisional meetings, and used this information as a starting point. Program directors were asked to relate their programs to the strategic priorities.

Existing services were subjected to the same internal and external feasibility analysis used in the selection of strategic priorities. Participants drew on information from the situational assessment survey and completed the same internal and external feasibility forms they had used earlier. Ideas for new, expanded, or enhanced services were discussed, as well as reductions or eliminations of current services that did not rate well against the feasibility factors.

In divisional meetings, staff members were asked to think about the following questions

- What more can be done to strengthen services or to deal with the service weaknesses you identified in the situational assessment survey?
- What service changes would increase access for clients?
- What, if any, structural or organizational changes would you make in your service?
- What service changes could you make that would save money?

Approximately 20 of the top managers and program directors then met to discuss this information and to brainstorm ideas for possible new services in line with the strategic priorities. This group produced a comprehensive list of 57 services or activities already offered by the agency pertinent to the strategic priorities and a second list of 57 relevant new service ideas.

The level of intervention—prevention, intervention, or remediation—was identified for existing and proposed services. The planning option called for if the idea was to be implemented—development, expansion, or enhancement—was also included, to make sure that the final plan would be a balance of new services and modified existing services. Areas for interdivisional and agencywide collaboration were identified and distinguished from efforts that could be made within each division.

The top management group met several more times, subjecting the items on the list to internal and external feasibility analyses to further reduce, or at least rank-order, the list of proposed services and activities. Existing services unrelated to the strategic priorities that rated poorly on the internal and external feasibility dimensions were earmarked for reduction or elimination.

Ultimately, the list of 57 new ideas was reduced to 21, of which 18 were primarily within divisions and three were major, interdivisional efforts requiring significant resources to develop and maintain. The three major initiatives proposed were an outpatient substance abuse treatment center, a day care center for a special-needs population of children, and a family preservation initiative for families in which removal of a child from the home was imminent or had already occurred. Details of the three major efforts were outlined. Each outline included a brief description, major objectives, staffing and space requirements, referral sources and linkages, and timelines for proposed activities over the next three years.

Similar information was provided on the 18 additional or smaller efforts within the divisions, including the level of intervention, the planning option employed, and the strategic priorities addressed.

The plan was approved by the board committee and then given final approval by the board as a whole.

In general, the development of this three-year action plan was guided by the knowledge that strategic planning is evolutionary rather than revolutionary, and that many of the problems targeted by the strategic priorities were interrelated and/or existed simultaneously. Innovation and risk-taking were encouraged, but tempered by consideration of the environment and other realities. Stakeholders—those who are affected by, or who influence, the future of the agency—were involved as fully as possible. Their participation was encouraged and results were shared with them both along the way and upon completion of the plan.

Monitoring the Plan

The board committee continued following the development of the plan through its monitoring and oversight role. To assess progress formally and periodically, the committee commissioned the agency's research and evaluation department to carry out the monitoring plan developed jointly by the department and the board committee. This collaboration assured that the results would fulfill the responsibilities of the board.

Monitoring took place at several levels. At the end of each year of the plan, an overall progress assessment was made in each of the strategic priority areas. The agency's research and evaluation department and the board committee developed a survey for top management and board members to use to rate progress on each of the strategic priorities as exceeding expectations, meeting expectations, partly meeting expectations, or not meeting expectations, with examples in support of their ratings. A general sense of progress was determined.

Progress on each of the three major initiatives was examined qualitatively from status reports and supporting narratives prepared by staff members involved in the effort and from oral presentations by top management. Staff members also formally reported on progress in each of the efforts within divisions. Each additional effort was rated on the scale described earlier: (1) have not yet started to address this activity; (2) are in the early planning/development stage; (3) are in an advanced stage of development and possible early implementation; (4) have implemented, accomplished, and/or completed the activity; or (5) chose to abandon the activity before implementation or accomplishment. Top management was asked to confirm or update information provided in the original plan, such as strategic priority addressed, planning option employed, and level of intervention.

Because some of these efforts required additional skills on the part of staff members, training related to the strategic priorities was planned and described in the monitoring report, along with a description of related, staff-directed community outreach, which was part of the agency's strategy. Since the agency's resources are limited, a list of activities or services that were reduced or eliminated in order to accomplish these new efforts was also provided by top management.

A less subjective type of monitoring was also attempted. Baseline data were gathered on the percentage of clients currently seen at the agency with primary problems related to one of the strategic priorities, as opposed to other problems, such as depression or marital difficulties. The same information was gathered annually to check shifts toward increased percentages of clients receiving treatment for problems in the strategic priority areas. Despite the difficulties with this monitoring technique outlined earlier, modest shifts were found in the anticipated direction.

The agency continues to modify its strategic plan annually as unanticipated changes and opportunities present themselves. The plan is a working document that is flexible enough to allow for refinements while providing overall direction for the agency.

References

Barry, B. W. (1986). *Strategic planning workbook for nonprofit organizations.* St. Paul, MN: Amherst H. Wilder Foundation.

Bryson, J. M. (1988). *Strategic planning for public and nonprofit organizations.* San Francisco: Jossey-Bass.

Delbecq, A. L., Van de Ven, A. H., & Gustafson, D. H. (1975). *Group techniques for program planning: A guide to Nominal Group and Delphi processes.* Glenview, IL: Scott-Foresman.

Drucker, P. F. (1973). *Management: Tasks, responsibilities, practices.* New York: Harper & Row.

Henderson, B. (1979). *Henderson on corporate strategy.* Cambridge, MA: University Press of America.

Moore, C. (1987). *Group techniques for idea building.* Newbury Park, CA: Sage Publications.

4

Assessing Outcome Effectiveness

Outcome effectiveness studies, also referred to as impact assessments [Rossi and Freeman 1989], offer a formal assessment of a service's efficacy. They measure whether a program has achieved its intended effects, realizing the goals that service staff members have set for their clients. It answers the question, does this service make a difference?

Because of the requirements of outside funders, many nonprofit organizations are increasingly being called upon to demonstrate the effectiveness of their services. The United Way, for example, requires organizations to demonstrate that the services it funds make a difference.

Advantages of an Outcome Effectiveness Study

In addition to funders' requirements, there are other reasons for outcome effectiveness studies. An organization's management and other staff members have an interest in knowing whether a service is effective. Outcome effectiveness identifies what services do well. When this confirms for staff members that their work is valued, burnout is reduced. The studies validate the hunches of top management and other staff members. And they remind management that accountability is essential to successfully running an organization, regardless of its profit/nonprofit status.

Outcome studies can demonstrate effectiveness in a quantifiable, objective manner that may be useful when applying for grants. Also, organizations that strive for excellence or total quality service find the studies valuable in improving services. Outcome effectiveness studies convey to clients that the organization cares about what

47

they think and wants to provide the best service possible. They both empower the client and give the agency the client's perspective for improving services.

How These Studies Differ from Other Approaches

Outcome effectiveness studies are unlike traditional program evaluations, which identify the strengths and weaknesses of a service. They are also unlike client satisfaction surveys, in which consumers are asked if they like or dislike services they are currently receiving. Although the studies may contain a client satisfaction component, they often have a more complex design than traditional program evaluations, requiring multiple measures from multiple sources, such as assessments of observable behaviors, clinical measures, and surveys.

Rather than relying on information provided solely by the client, as a client satisfaction survey does, these studies often seek information from the service provider as well. Because no one source of information holds the definitive answer on whether the service has been effective, the multiple measures of the studies must come from as many sources as possible. The studies also focus on outcome rather than process, to determine whether the client has improved in a way targeted by the service. This focus may lead to lengthy studies to collect information at intervals or at the completion of service. Information may also be collected several weeks, months, or even years after receipt of services to determine how permanent any positive outcomes may have been.

Characteristics of an Outcome Effectiveness Study

In comparison with other kinds of evaluations or assessments, outcome effectiveness studies tend to take more time for those who conduct them to plan. At the authors' agency, using staff member evaluators, the study took almost two years to complete. A shift from accounting for process factors, such as units of service delivered, to an outcome orientation often takes a good deal of time. Outcomes are more difficult to measure than units of service. No accounting systems are in place to gather this type of information, and there is rarely, if ever, one objective measure of effectiveness.

Further, perspectives often differ on what it means for a particular service to be effective. Staff members may confuse outcome effectiveness with process, defining what they do rather than what they hope to accomplish.

A template for conducting outcome effectiveness studies has emerged from the authors' experiences. Its key components are a team approach, a definition of effectiveness, multiple measures of effectiveness, and sensitivity to the practitioner's perspective.

Team Approach

As with any research or evaluation study at the Village for Families and Children, the study took a team approach. For strong planning, representatives from the research side and the service side must work collaboratively in the design and implementation of the study. Each brings a particular perspective and has a particular expertise. Researchers have technological expertise in survey development, while service providers know about clinical issues that have bearing on the instrument to be developed. A collaborative approach to design and implementation yields a process that is doable and a product that is useful to practitioners and managers.

For this collaborative team to function smoothly, however, roles and responsibilities must be clearly designated. Who has the ultimate responsibility for each aspect of the study? Ideally the researchers and practitioners arrive at mutually satisfactory decisions through consensus. If an issue is unresolved, however, it must be clear who has ultimate authority over that aspect of the study.

A team of three to four staff members is ideal. If too many staff members are in the group, it becomes difficult to find mutually agreeable times to schedule meetings. Decision-making may also slow to a crawl when there are too many viewpoints. Alternatively, too few staff members on a team may limit exposure to different perspectives and the focus may be narrow or incomplete.

Fortunately, there are ways to receive opinions from a cross-section of the staff without increasing the team size, such as inviting suggestions from other staff members via memos and occasional large group meetings to share progress and solicit ideas. Team members may also act as representatives, asking coworkers for their reactions to ideas and providing them with updates.

Team meetings are necessary to plan the study. They engage service providers in the process and foster a sense of ownership. Research staff members also benefit by gaining a better understanding of service issues. All team members should be involved in the development and selection of measures and in design, and be available to discuss results and their interpretation.

Definition of Effectiveness

One of the first steps and foremost considerations in an outcome study is defining effectiveness clearly and accurately. Different philosophical frameworks and viewpoints influence what is viewed as the ideal goal or outcome of a service. A key ingredient in defining effectiveness, then, is mutual agreement among practitioners and between researchers and practitioners.

Printed materials such as brochures, announcements, and studies prepared for accreditation or licensure can shed light on the mission, purpose, and goals of the service. Interviews with staff members can provide additional information, as unwritten service philosophies may have evolved over time.

This stage of the study can take from two to four months. If team members are not involved in a thorough analysis, an incomplete or inaccurate definition will be developed that will ultimately cast doubt on the validity of the entire study. The process of defining effectiveness for a particular service can be grueling and frustrating, but it is a necessary component that cannot be rushed.

Multiple Measures

Outcome effectiveness is not one concise variable that is easily measured. There is no single, all-encompassing, objective source. The best approximation combines information from as many sources as possible. This calls for a diligent effort.

Service providers are an ideal and ever-present source of information. They are in daily contact with the clients and they continually observe change through experienced eyes. To some extent, however, their perceptions may be subjective. They will be influenced by their training orientation and by their individual standards or thresholds in acknowledging change. This is one reason for the importance of a uniform definition of effectiveness that is accepted by all the service providers.

The providers' judgment of effectiveness may also be influenced, consciously or unconsciously, by the desire to have personally made a difference in clients' lives. Providers want their efforts to be validated. Some also want to look good to their supervisors and/or peers, causing their assessments to be more positive and optimistic than is actually warranted.

Clients are another key source of information. Regardless of how providers rate effectiveness of service, clients have their own views on whether the services they received made a difference. But like the providers' responses, the responses of clients are influenced by various factors, such as a desire to give what they perceive to be the right answers. Their "right answers" validate the time and effort they have given to obtain services. They may also have a desire to please their provider, despite being assured of the confidentiality of their responses. Clients may be receiving services in a time of crisis and great need, and may not respond or judge as accurately as they might during a less difficult time. Further, if the services being received contain a mental health component, a temporary intensification of problems or feelings may be seen as progress by the service provider, but seen as a step backward by the client.

Other sources of information are agency bookkeeping records and clients' records. Documentation on appointment-keeping, for example, may contribute to the overall picture of service effectiveness. Other observable forms of information include improvement in a parent's employment status, reunification of a biological family whose child had been placed outside the home, and maintenance of a placement at risk of disrupting.

People in ancillary or collateral roles may also contribute useful information. A teacher may provide information on changes observed in the classroom concomitant with service at the agency.

While evaluators hope to assemble assessments of service effectiveness for a particular individual that agree with each other, the points of divergence are also of interest. They can lead to a greater understanding of the client's perspective across all the levels of the organization's staff, and offer encouragement and validation for any providers who rated their effectiveness lower than did their clients. Some providers will have to reassess treatments and question automatic, long-standing assumptions if their ratings are routinely higher than their clients' ratings.

Another consideration is worth noting with regard to assessment of service effectiveness. Suppose that clients receiving services change in the anticipated, hoped-for direction. Before one can conclude that the service received is the source of this outcome, other extenuating circumstances or factors must be examined. For example, the improvement may have been caused by a positive change in the client's home environment or employment circumstances, or by a service provided by some other nonprofit organization or community resource, such as a faith community or self-help group. One way to anticipate contributing factors and build them into the collection of information is to ask clients to rate how various factors on a list (including the service being assessed) contributed to their progress. This list of possible contributing factors should be assembled early in discussions of the study design so that appropriate information may be collected.

Sensitivity to the Practitioner

Service providers are often concerned that information collected during the study may be shared with supervisors or top management and used punitively. It is crucial to affirm that findings will be presented only in the aggregate, and individual responses will not be linked and presented in study reports. It is true, of course, that effectiveness is influenced by the service provider's skills, but lack of such assurances will lead to a defensive posture, particularly among those who have not played an active role in the study's development. Besides, if there is a performance problem involving any of the service providers, a study will not be required to uncover it. More than likely the problem is already known and can be addressed by his or her supervisor.

Any supervisor who is tempted to request clients' ratings of an individual service provider should be reminded that this is a supervisory matter, and that valid findings cannot be obtained from the study if information sources do not feel secure enough to respond freely and without fear of consequences.

Why Gather Both Kinds of Information?

There are several good reasons why the service provider-client data linkage, while threatening, should nevertheless be made. As described earlier, assessment of outcome effectiveness is complex, and many of the sources of information are flawed or biased. The more viewpoints gathered, therefore, the better the opportunity to determine the actual effectiveness of a service.

Including both service provider and client viewpoints encourages staff involvement in the study and commitment to providing quality service. Clients may not always be aware of changes in their behavior that the service provider notices. In addition, not every client solicited for the study may choose to participate, leading to a selection bias and results that are not necessarily representative or generalizable. Clients ordered by the courts to receive services, for example, may be unwilling to participate in the study. The same may be true of dissatisfied clients.

Some clients may want to participate, but be unable to do so because of a literacy problem or difficulty in understanding the questions being asked. In such cases, service provider assessments may be the only source of information on the group of clients being recruited for the study. In addition, if the service is mental health related, such as psychotherapy for troubled youngsters, completion of relevant scales by service providers may be a substitute or alternative to clinical testing.

Linking the service provider and client ratings makes the characteristics of the most successful matches apparent and available to be used in future assignments of clients to service providers. It may give service directors information that can help in future staff recruitment efforts. It also provides a mechanism for confidentially reporting back to the service provider an aggregate or summary of information given by his or her clients. This personalizing of the findings may enable the staff member to make changes in his or her delivery of service.

In particularly sensitive study areas, however, anonymity may be the only way to gather useful information directly from clients. Outcome effectiveness studies that include assessments of illegal drug use, alcohol consumption among adolescents, or criminal behavior, for example, may be particularly likely to receive only socially desirable responses from clients. This information, if known for a particular client, may also be subpoenaed as evidence by law officials, thus putting study participants at risk of being identified.

To sum up, it is crucial to gather information from both the service provider and the client, and, ideally, to be able to link both pieces of information. When concern about linking these data sources arises, the researcher must educate or remind the parties about the purpose of the study. Participants must also be guaranteed that the findings will be presented only in the aggregate and that immediate supervisors and top management will not have access to individual client ratings, or even aggregate ratings for a particular service provider.

Other Considerations

It is important to explain that all information collected will be kept in a locked file, no names will ever be entered into a computer for research purposes, and only the researchers will have access to the lists that match clients with their service providers. Again, service providers must understand that gaining a full perspective requires multiple sources of information, including any important factors contributing to service effectiveness.

There may also be concern that negative findings, that is, lack of evidence for the efficacy of a service, will lead to the service's demise. To the extent possible, the reasons for doing the outcome effectiveness study and the proposed ways in which the results will be used should be explained or re-explained to service providers.

Clients, as well as service providers, must be assured and reassured of confidentiality. To be as candid as possible in the information they provide, clients must believe that their individual answers will not be shared with their service providers. Client participants must understand the general purpose of the study and how information they offer is safeguarded, including keeping it in a locked drawer and not entering their names into a computer. Clients participating may also have the opportunity to receive a copy of the general findings at completion of the study.

One final issue that often arises in outcome effectiveness studies is the extra work time it will take for the service providers who participate in such a study. This point is a valid one, particularly for the often overworked staff members of nonprofit organizations. Service directors and top management should acknowledge the extra effort required, while at the same time reinforcing the importance and the benefits of doing such studies. Cooperation must be recognized formally and informally, and data collection procedures and instruments must be designed to be as unobtrusive and quick to complete as possible.

Summary of Steps Taken in Conducting an Outcome Effectiveness Study

Each outcome effectiveness study should include certain steps that take place in a particular order.

Step 1. Form the Study Team

Since services are examined individually in this model, a multiservice organization must select which ones will be studied. Is a particular service funded by an organization that requires an outcome effectiveness study? Is there a particular service that would like to apply for a large grant and could help its case by having solid information about its effectiveness?

Because outcome effectiveness studies require many hours over an extended period, another consideration when selecting which service to assess is the time availability of the service director and the service staff. Usually the service director and one or two other service providers will be on the team, along with a head researcher and perhaps a research assistant (who might be a student intern or college volunteer). A tentative meeting schedule would be drawn up and plans made to communicate the team's progress in designing the outcome effectiveness study.

Step 2. Define Outcome Effectiveness

Once the service to be studied has been identified and the team formed, service effectiveness must be defined. Individual ideas related to effectiveness may be generated, perhaps starting with a brainstorming session. Relevant information may also be extracted from printed service material. Research staff may find it helpful to interview staff members in the service being studied. The result should be a clear, concise, unanimous definition of what effectiveness means for this service.

Step 3. Design the Study

Once the definition of service effectiveness has been written and agreed to, the team members must ask themselves how they will know whether this definition has been fulfilled. It will almost always be the case that multiple measures are required from two or more sources. Standardized scales or surveys may meet the needs of the study, or perhaps a structured interview is required. Case records, if available, may be another source of information. Computerized case records or bookkeeping information may be a source to consider when finding objective ways to assess outcome effectiveness. People in ancillary or collateral roles, such as teachers, are yet another potential source of information.

The team must balance its enthusiasm for including many measures in its study with realistic time demands on the study participants, researchers collecting the information, and any other staff members required to provide information.

Timelines should be developed for such possible activities as

- developing consent forms to be completed by clients
- piloting of new instruments
- obtaining Spanish (or other language) translations of instruments and consent forms to be completed by clients not fluent in English
- running a trial of the study protocol, including all data collection procedures, for possible revision before the official data collection period of the study
- establishing a formal data collection period

- planning to notify potential participants about the study before requesting their participation
- devising systems for coding the information gathered, if necessary
- entering computer data, if required
- analyzing the information provided
- reviewing preliminary results as a team
- conducting further analysis
- reviewing further analyses and implications as a team
- writing the report
- sharing findings with top management, service providers, and others involved in the study, including clients

Step 4. Collect Study Information

A way of notifying participants about the study must be developed before their participation is requested. A notification period before beginning the actual collection of information allows the clients time to decide whether they want to participate and to ask their service provider or a research staff member any questions they have about the study.

After the data collection instruments and procedures have been tried out with a small group of those soon to be asked to participate in the study, revisions made, and another tryout done, if indicated, the formal collection of study information begins.

The time needed for data collection depends on how the study has been designed. For example, a very brief period of time, as little as a week, could be selected, and service effectiveness assessed for all clients seen during that one-week period. The information may take longer to collect if clients must have completed receipt of service before outcome effectiveness is assessed. Another possible study design requires assessments of effectiveness six months after service delivery has ended.

Step 5. Analyze Information Collected

When the information has been collected, it must be analyzed. Information may be coded into categories before being entered into the computer. Frequently, a preliminary analysis is done and the findings reviewed by the team. Interpretation of the findings leads to asking new questions to support or disprove possible explanations.

The next round of analysis is carried out and the results shared with the team. This iterative analysis-review-further analysis process may go on for an extended period of time before all team members are satisfied that the findings have been explained as fully as possible.

Step 6. Share Findings

A written report is produced that explains why the outcome effectiveness study was done, how effectiveness was defined, who participated in the study, how the information was collected, what the findings were, and how the findings were interpreted. In studies that call for the collection of information at multiple points, or include a follow-up period some time after service has been completed, the issuing of interim reports may be appropriate.

The information should also be summarized in a brief overview for those who will not read the full report. A brief written report should be sent to clients and any others who participated in the study. Individual reports may also be prepared for service providers, summarizing findings for their clients.

Oral presentations of the study may be given at meetings of staff members, of top management, of the full organization, and of the board. On a professional level, information may also be shared at conferences and in journal articles.

Example of an Outcome Effectiveness Study at the Village for Families and Children

Interest had surfaced several years before the implementation of the Village for Families and Children's first outcome effectiveness study. When one of the agency's funders, the United Way, made this a requirement, the impetus for the effort solidified. At the time of this writing, the Village for Families and Children has completed or initiated five outcome effectiveness studies. The experience has been helpful in a variety of ways, and despite the cost, top management is committed to continuing the studies.

One outcome effectiveness study was recently completed in the agency's family day care program [Mika et al. 1991]. This program provides affordable care for infants and children whose parents are out of the home due to employment, job training, or education. Licensed family day care providers are carefully selected, trained, and supervised by a professional staff member. The agency offers social worker support, handles collection of payment from the parents, and facilitates parent support groups.

The original study team consisted of two research staff members and two service directors (in urban and suburban offices) in charge of the agency's two family day care programs. Due to the relocation of one of the service directors and maternity leave for one of the researchers, the team configuration was modified somewhat. The six social workers in the urban family day care setting all worked with the research staff member and the service director from the suburban office. Together, over several months, they developed a definition of effectiveness for the family day care service. Family day care services are effective when children are placed in homes that provide consistent and interesting days, including

- appropriate physical care;
- nurturing emotional development;
- communication among parent, provider, and social worker; and
- planned activities to encourage social, physical, and cognitive growth.

A subgroup of the larger group that worked on the effectiveness definition extended their involvement to designing the study. Study activities were listed and timelines developed.

Questions pertinent to the four elements of the definition were developed and surveys were tried out with day care providers, parents, and professional staff members. Unfortunately, the children in the day care homes could not be interviewed within the time and budget constraints of the study. One complication was that the children varied in age from infants to ten-year-olds, and no uniform assessment could be used for this age range.

Following a letter notifying the day care providers of the study, information was collected from all 37 via telephone interviews conducted by research staff members. In regard to appropriate physical care, for example, the family day care providers were asked about scheduled rest times and about encouragement of good hygiene habits for the children. Questions about emotional nurturing included how often they expressed affection and praised the child. Their communication with parents was assessed through questions such as how often they spoke to parents about their child's day and how they collaborated with parents in problem-solving. Other questions concerned the frequency of planned activities, such as arts and crafts, reading, puzzles, and outdoor play.

The 96 parents were sent a notification letter before the study. All were reached by telephone and agreed to be interviewed by the agency researcher. Parents, like day care providers, answered questions in the four areas outlined in the definition. To assess appropriate physical care, for example, parents were asked whether they thought the day care provider had safety rules for the child to follow and whether there was an opportunity for the child to nap each day. As to emotional nurturing, parents were asked how often the day care provider praised, comforted, and listened to the child. Communication-related questions included the degree of respect the day care provider showed for the parent's beliefs about child-rearing and the frequency of discussions about the child's learning of new skills. Parents were also asked how frequently they thought various activities, such as arts and crafts, play dough, and puzzles, were scheduled.

The third source of information was the agency social workers assigned to these cases. Using questionnaires, they rated each child and his or her day care home in the four areas. In addition to the questions asked of the day care providers and parents, social workers were also asked about the day care provider's knowledge of nutrition and ability to handle emergencies. Questions assessing emotional nurturing rated the day care providers on demonstrated knowledge of socio-emotional growth in children and effective discipline techniques. Questions about communication included the social worker's perception of how well the provider could discuss sensitive matters with parents and whether the social worker ever had to intervene to settle difficulties between parents and day care providers. Regarding planned activities, the social workers were asked to rate the day care providers on their knowledge of child development, which would affect the kind of activities engaged in during child care, and on such items as knowledge of learning skills and age-appropriate toys and games.

After this information was gathered, coded, and entered into a computer, team members discussed the preliminary analyses and their interpretation. Further analysis resulted in a 400-page final report. The information was also summarized in a brief report sent to day care providers and parents. The findings were presented at service and divisional meetings, at a meeting of the full board of directors, and at professional conferences.

In general, the study found the agency family day care program to be effective. All four areas of the effectiveness definition were present to the high satisfaction of the parents, day care providers, and social workers. The following were among the key findings

- Day care providers offer warm and nurturing environments for the children.
- The day care homes offer a wide range of activities that reinforce developmental skills.
- The variety of scheduled activities is not uniform across the day care homes; some children may be missing stimulating experiences.
- Social workers rated the day care providers' physical care skills somewhat lower than did the parents and day care providers themselves, suggesting potential areas for improvement.
- Although parents indicated their satisfaction, the day care providers thought more communication was needed to heighten the quality of care.

Thus, the findings showed the agency's family day care service to be effective and also found some areas for improvement. Several changes occurred as a result of this study. For example, an article was published in the agency's newsletter for parents on how to talk to a day care provider about the child's day. Parent support groups were formed, and the CPR/first aid training routinely given to day care providers was extended to parents.

Outcome effectiveness studies will continue to play an integral role at the Village for Families and Children, as the organization strives to provide an ever higher quality of service to its clients.

References

Mika, K. L., Kluger, M. P., & Aprea, D. M. (September 1991). *Outcome effectiveness study of family day care services.* Hartford, CT: Child and Family Services, Inc.

Rossi, P. H., & Freeman, H. E. (1989). *Evaluation: A systematic approach* (4th ed.). Newbury Park, CA: Sage Publications.

5

Assessing the Health of the Nonprofit Organization

Why should top management be concerned about the health of their nonprofit agency? First, because the health of an organization, particularly a service-delivery organization, influences the quality of the services that consumers and clients receive [James and Jones 1976; Schneider et al. 1980]. If quality declines and other providers are available, current and/or potential clients will turn to the competition. This will have an impact on future revenues that might have been received from public or private funding sources and from some clients. Income reductions, of course, threaten the viability of the organization.

Even if a nonprofit organization offers the only such service in the community, responsible leaders in that organization will still try to serve clients and consumers to the best of their ability. The highest quality service or product can be delivered only when morale is high, the leadership and the staff are enthusiastic and committed to the work they do, and staff members have a sense of camaraderie, cooperation, and collaborative effort. When service providers feel valued, they convey that positive feeling to clients, who will then receive better services or products.

From management's perspective, reduced staff turnover is another benefit of a healthy climate. The time needed to recruit and train new employees is minimized, and disruption of productivity and its impact on clients are diminished. Although turnover can be healthy for an organization when new ideas and experiences are introduced, uncontrolled, unanticipated turnover, particularly of key employees, can seriously harm the work environment. In a nonprofit organization, particularly a small one, job satisfaction or dissatisfaction can have significant and widespread ramifications. Frequent and unexpected management and staff turnover also sends a negative message to the remaining employees: This is not a great place to work; you may want to find a job elsewhere, too.

Top management of nonprofit organizations should be particularly concerned about organizational well-being when major changes have recently taken place or are in the offing. In this context, a health assessment can measure the impact of change. Depending on the kind of change, it can also provide feedback to the leadership on how well they did their jobs. Was the change handled in the best way possible, or has the general morale of the organization unnecessarily plummeted? If health is assessed periodically, and a downward trend is noted, top management can deal promptly with particular problems. Future health assessments will provide further feedback on whether staff perceptions, attitudes, morale, and so on have improved.

Sometimes no major changes can be identified, but management has a hunch or a gut feeling that the atmosphere at the organization is changing. An assessment can confirm these hunches, and may shed light on the causes of any shift in staff morale. If the organization's leaders have contrasting hunches or opinions, a formal assessment may resolve the impasse. The process may also yield surprising new information.

If an organization is not particularly open and friendly, staff members may be reluctant to voice concern to top management for fear of retribution. They may simply feel that rapport is lacking and frank discussions with supervisors would be uncomfortable. It is important for the staff to have formal, confidential channels for communicating concern. Offhand remarks about a particular internal matter may have a cumulative effect over time, yet not be given the serious attention they deserve until agencywide concern is clear.

Some staff members may be frustrated by a belief that they are not heard by top management. An organizational health assessment may alleviate the frustration, particularly if managers communicate ways in which the study results will lead to changes. One note of caution: Some employees may equate publicizing of staff suggestions with a decision by top leadership to implement those suggestions. The staff must understand that an organization cannot be directed solely by a survey.

When the operation is openly critiqued, top management can learn what staff members see as the strengths and weaknesses of their organization. Taking the organization's temperature periodically heightens receptivity to particular changes, so events may be anticipated and planned for accordingly. The assessment may, therefore, have a subtle effect on an organization's operation and decision-making. With further thought and a review of available information, management may, for example, deal directly with a problem that has been raised. A change in policy or procedures may emerge. Further assessments can indicate whether the new strategy effected a positive change and led to an improvement in the agency's climate.

When assessment is routine, a monitoring-feedback loop is created for top management's efforts to improve the organization. The process may concentrate on particular weaknesses, but special strengths that can be capitalized upon may also be highlighted, and then emphasized during recruitment for vacant positions and student interns.

To summarize, a healthy climate is a prerequisite for producing the best possible service or product while saving time and money for the organization.

A Model for Assessing Organizational Health

How can an organization's health be assessed? The first step is to find a way to conduct a checkup as fairly and objectively as possible. The following is one model for a periodic survey of the health of an organization.

Step 1. Develop the Instrument

Every organization is unique, so any methodology for assessing organizational health must be tailored to the particular setting. Regardless of the setting, however, one person, team, or department must be designated to lead the assessment. Depending on the size of the organization, focus groups and/or individual interviews may be held to determine content areas for inclusion in the survey, chiefly related to the agency's services, management, and employees. Questions can then be developed that tap into the respondents' attitudes, level of satisfaction, and/or knowledge or perceptions in given areas.

Services/Products

Depending on the purpose of the organization, questions can be developed to assess

- understanding of the organization's mission, policies, and strategic plans
- professional and community perceptions of the organization

- judgment of the quality of service clients receive
- nature and degree of staff members' respect for clients
- timeliness of service to clients
- perception of clients' satisfaction with the physical environment where service is given
- competitiveness of organization to attract and retain clients

Management

Although management is not an exercise in popularity, it is important for top managers, the leaders of the organization, to be respected by their employees. A well-respected leader will encourage staff members to put forth their best efforts, a prerequisite for quality service delivery and a healthy climate. Appropriate survey items in this area may include

- understanding of, and concurrence with, management's philosophy and vision
- overall efficiency and effectiveness of management
- clarity and timeliness of administrative communications
- timeliness of management decision-making
- comfort in discussing difficulties and concerns with management
- satisfaction with the timeliness and content of management's response to staff members
- adequacy of opportunities for staff members to develop new skills/professional identities
- encouragement of employees' creativity and innovation
- satisfaction with handling of performance reviews and grievance procedures
- flexibility of policies
- perceived morale level of leadership and supervisors

Employees

Staff members' perceptions, attitudes, and satisfaction strongly affect performance and influence the organization's climate. Questions can range over a variety of considerations to assess

- level of enthusiasm about working at the organization
- pride in being associated with the organization
- staff members' commitment to a common purpose or common goals
- level of employee morale

- whether staff members like, and are committed to, their jobs
- whether staff members feel like valued employees, and are recognized as such
- quality of internal services (such as bookkeeping, maintenance) and interactions
- degree of employee respect for other employees of the organization
- whether employees enjoy and work well with staff members from other divisions
- job-market competitiveness of salaries and benefits
- ability to attract and retain qualified, competent, and committed staff members
- thoroughness of employee orientation
- incentives for excellence as an inherent part of the organization
- workloads and job stress levels

Responses to items should accord with a rating scale of at least four points; a six-point scale is ideal [Nunnally 1978]. Items might be phrased to require a frequency rating of always, often, sometimes, occasionally, rarely, or never, or the format might require respondents to express a level of agreement on a particular topic ranging from strongly agree to strongly disagree.

Numerical ratings lend themselves to comparisons of items and areas. If the same questions are repeated in a future survey, comparisons of scores will be useful in assessing progress, new problem areas, and so forth. An overall composite or climate score can also be computed from numerical responses. Other information important to capture for use in analyzing responses may include

- unit, service, or division,
- number of years with the organization,
- job level, and
- job function or type.

In addition to numerical (closed-end) ratings, the instrument should also include open-ended items that allow respondents to comment on particular strengths and weaknesses of the organization's services, management, staff, or other areas not covered in the survey. These replies may suggest areas to be queried in a future survey, as well as creative solutions to problems.

Step 2. Collect Data

Survey Distribution

It would be ideal to offer all the organization's employees an opportunity to respond to the survey and express their sentiments. If this is not feasible, due, for example, to a large number of staff members, a random sampling can be done by surveying a certain percentage of the organization's staff in a given arena. A stratified sample will ensure organizational representativeness. A percentage of the staff members may be randomly selected from each unit or job level to receive a survey [see Chadhuri and Stenger 1992; Peterson 1988].

The employees who will be surveyed should be informed about the survey before receiving it in the mail, perhaps through the organization's newsletter, memos, staff meetings, or voice mail broadcasts. When the survey is mailed, it should be accompanied by a memo or letter (re)stating the purpose of the survey, top management's support for it, its confidentiality, and the deadline for the surveys to be returned. A contact person for any questions should also be included, preferably the researcher.

Confidentiality

First, to accurately assess the organization's climate, staff responses have to be as candid as possible. Second, a large response rate that yields a representative sample of attitudes and perceptions is also necessary. One of the conditions for sufficient and useful responses is an assurance of confidentiality. Confidentiality has been defined as a situation in which the researcher has the capability to identify a subject's responses but essentially promises not to do so [Babbie 1983].

Anonymity must also be considered. Anonymity is defined as a situation in which the respondent is unknown to or can't be identified by the researcher [Babbie 1983]. In a survey that contains some sensitive questions, anonymity has the advantage of encouraging respondents to be candid. Otherwise, despite assurances to the contrary, some staff members may be suspicious, fearing that their negative responses will not be kept confidential, will be shared with their supervisors or top management, and will result in punitive actions toward them personally.

While anonymity eliminates the element of pressure or coercion to participate in the study, it may also lead to a low, nonrepresentative response rate. Perhaps only those feeling positive about the organization will respond, or perhaps more of the staff members who feel negative toward the organization will take the opportunity to respond. Whatever the reason, the results cannot validly be generalized to the entire staff. Bad or misleading information may be worse than no information.

Anonymity also avoids the subtle pressure of at least one other person—the researcher—knowing whether or not recipients responded, but it makes it impossible to follow up nonrespondents [Mika and Kluger 1990]. Because mailed surveys often have a low return rate [Fowler 1988], a follow-up contact, usually in the form of a letter, is often essential [Sudman, 1976]. The authors, therefore, recommend a confidential rather than an anonymous survey.

Presenting the Survey

Whoever commissions or sanctions the collection of data to assess organizational health must convey support for the effort to those asked to participate in the study. The top manager—the executive director or president of the organization—or the top management group, in announcing the study, should address the question of confidentiality. They can stress that everyone's opinion is valued, and that everyone's participation is necessary for a clear picture of all the staff members' attitudes and perceptions of the organization. This message must be reiterated in the instructions that accompany the survey.

As an added incentive to participation, it is important to let potential study respondents know that the findings will be shared with them when a final report is completed. This will allow staff members to learn more about the organization. Employees can then know, for example, how the majority of the staff members feel about top management, other staff members, and the organization as a whole. This may either validate their perceptions or suggest that their positive or negative feelings are not generally shared and may stem from their particular situation.

To further encourage staff member participation, top management and researchers must point out that all information will be reported in the aggregate, that is, in a summarized format. Individual responses will not be identified or shared with supervisors or anyone else in a position of authority, and no punitive action will follow from any answer. Further, all data will be kept in a locked file drawer and no staff names will be entered onto any computer data file. Respondents must trust that researchers and administration will honor these commitments.

Step 3. Analyze and Interpret Results

The data can be summarized in several ways. To begin, the answers to each survey item can be examined separately. By totaling the responses to a statement about the organization (strongly agree, agree, somewhat agree, somewhat disagree, disagree, strongly disagree), the researcher can calculate what percentage of the staff gave what rating. Let us say that 20% of the respondents strongly agreed that they have adequate opportunities to develop new skills, 50% agreed, 20% somewhat agreed, and 10% strongly disagreed. An average rating, usually the arithmetic mean, can be calculated by way of summary.

Once individual items have been analyzed separately, they can be put into context by comparing responses from one item to another. On the basis of the calculated averages, the items can be re-ordered from the most to the least favorable ratings. The leadership then has a sense of which areas need more attention than others. An overall composite or climate score can also be obtained by averaging all the item averages.

If the same survey has been conducted previously, results can be compared from year to year. The researcher would analyze whether or not the differences in percentages or averages over time represent a statistically significant change. Tangible improvements may be measured by higher staff ratings—a reinforcement for top managers, who sometimes recall or focus on the negative rather than the positive. Has the level of enthusiasm about working at the organization increased, for instance? Has the perceived timeliness of administrative communications dropped significantly?

Comparisons may also be made between different groups of employees. In the earlier example of responses to a statement about opportunities to develop new skills, all but 10% of the respondents gave somewhat positive to very positive answers. This 10% of employees were at the extreme negative end of the rating scale, disagreeing strongly that adequate opportunities to develop new skills were available. Is the majority of this group in one particular type of job at the organization? An analysis that compares responses given by groups of staff members in particular jobs would answer that question. Have the majority of the 10% group been with the organization for a long time, so they are its most experienced or seasoned employees? An analysis that relates response to the statement with length of service would supply an answer.

It is important for analyses contrasting one group of staff members with another to contain numbers large enough to prevent a reader from guessing the identity of a particular individual from the reported results. Reporting differences in staff responses between units would not be acceptable if any of the units had only one or two staff members, so it would be easy to identify who said what. If group sizes are sufficient, however, these comparative analyses can yield important information for the organization's leadership.

To carry the example one step further: Suppose the previously suggested analyses showed that nearly all the employees who strongly denied the adequacy of opportunities to develop new skills were clerical staff members. A training program to enhance word processing skills might then be created. The following year the organization's climate might be reassessed, the same survey distributed, and responses analyzed. The new results could help leadership determine whether an improvement had taken place for this group. Results could even have generalized to more positive ratings by the clerical staff in other areas.

Step 4. Report the Results

As noted earlier, the results should be presented in a way that protects respondent confidentiality. No findings should be reported that can be clearly traced to particular individuals. The full report of findings should first be given to those who commissioned the assessment of the organization's health. The next step would be to provide a summary of the findings to all employees through staff newsletters, meetings, and other means. It is especially important for study participants to receive a summary of the findings and of future actions, if any, that will occur as a result of this assessment.

The Experience of the Village for Families and Children

Prompted by a general sense of staff member dissatisfaction, top management at the Village for Families and Children decided to formally assess the state of the organization's health. Before this undertaking, the agency's top management had no overall quantifiable measurement of staff perceptions of life at the agency. Every organization has members who are more vocal than others. Did the vocal members represent majority opinion about the top management, other staff members, and the agency as a whole? Were there aspects of management that could be improved?

A 24-item survey based on suggestions from the agency's top management was developed and distributed to all 150 staff members. Questions covered such topics as staff member awareness of the agency's purpose, agency philosophy, adequacy of communication patterns, top management's decision-making, and treatment of staff members. A five-point rating scale was used for each of the statements. Points on the scale were always, often, sometimes, seldom, and never. The survey asked such questions as the following

- Do you feel that top management's decisions are made in a timely manner?
- As a staff member of this agency, do you feel valued?
- Are the salaries the agency offers competitive?
- Do administrators encourage employee creativity and innovation?
- Do you think about leaving the agency?
- Do staff members have the competence to deliver superior performance?

The arithmetic mean, or average, was calculated for each item on the survey, and an overall composite score was determined. As of this writing, the survey has been conducted annually for three years to encompass changes over time. The first two surveys were anonymous, and as is typical, the return rate was low, with slightly better than one-third of the staff responding. For the most recent survey, however, the protocol was changed to assure confidentiality, not anonymity. By assigning identification numbers to surveys, the researcher was able to track which staff members had responded. A follow-up to nonrespondents included a reminder note and a second copy of the survey. The final return rate was a much-improved 74%.

Results were shared with all 150 staff members, and there was a general sense of gratitude for the opportunity to express opinions to top management. The results were used in several ways. After the initial survey, the agency's top management reviewed the findings and discussed potential actions to be taken to remedy weaknesses. Several changes were made almost immediately. For example, the staff frequently criticized the agency's top management for not being open and communicative. In response, the top management decided to publish its meeting agendas in the weekly staff newsletter. Lack of opportunity for staff input was another point raised in the findings. In response, the top management of the agency scheduled regular office hours during which any staff member could stop by to discuss any issue.

A new salary program was also implemented, based in part on overall staff member perception that current salaries were not competitive. Other subtle changes occurred over time that top management, in retrospect, traced to the surveys' findings. For example, top managers became more sensitive to the value of soliciting staff member suggestions and involving staff committees in various agency developments. Top management also made a concerted effort to communicate more information regarding their decisions.

Trends were examined over time, particularly where efforts to bring about improvement had been made. In general, modest changes in staff responses emerged the second and third times the survey was given. Average ratings rose significantly for a few of the survey items. One increase, for example, derived from the emphasis given throughout the organization to the agency's commitment to a common purpose and its competence to deliver superior performance.

Several benefits attest to the value of formally assessing the agency's health. In general, top management's understanding of the staff members' views has improved. Tangible improvement has been quantified by higher staff member ratings over time. The survey itself has met the staff members' desire for an avenue to express their concerns. Staff members have also gained a better understanding of how the majority of agency employees feel about top management, other staff members, and the organization in general.

The survey revealed an important diversity of opinions and values held by employees. Some staff members place value on quick decision-making, for example, while others favor taking time for a process that includes staff input. Although it would be nearly impossible for the agency's top management to satisfy both viewpoints, the findings clarify some value conflicts that must be understood, accepted, and managed. Realistically, someone will almost always be unhappy about an action or change that delights someone else.

The existence of these conflicting points of view is confirmation that the agency's climate is healthy and vibrant. Disaster would surely follow if all decisions were made quickly and without diverse input. Similarly, the agency would be strangled if no decision could be made until exhaustive input had been gathered.

During discussion of the findings from the most recent survey, the top management suggested that further analyses be conducted concerning seniority and negative attitudes. In addition to number of years at the agency, job level differences and differences among service divisions were also analyzed. The results confirmed some of top management's hunches, but did not support other hunches, and yielded several surprises as well.

Because the results of the last two surveys were similar, it was decided to conduct the survey biennially in the future. Since the confidential, but not anonymous protocol caused a striking increase in staff member participation, it will be continued for future surveys. Information from staff members continues to be valued, however, so a focused survey will be conducted during the off years. These surveys will narrow their questions to a particular project, change, or issue. For example, the agency recently assessed staff satisfaction with a newly automated and centralized client intake and fee setting system. Staff suggestion boxes were placed in high-traffic areas throughout the agency, and a procedure for handling the suggestions was developed.

In summary, the Village for Families and Children's top management found the assessment of its organization's climate to yield useful management information. Several agency changes can be traced directly or indirectly to these surveys. Overall, the staff members seemed to appreciate and welcome this opportunity to confidentially offer their views on various aspects of life at the agency. Organizational health will remain important to top management in the coming years as changes continue to take place.

References

Babbie, E. (1983). *The practice of social research.* Belmont, CA: Wadsworth.

Chadhuri, A., & Stenger, H. (1992). *Survey sampling: Theory and methods.* New York: Marcel Dekker.

Fowler, F. (1988). *Survey research methods.* Newbury Park, CA: Sage.

James, L. R., & Jones, A. P. (1976). Organizational structure: A review of structural dimensions and their conceptual relationships with individual attitudes and behavior. *Organizational Behavior and Human Performance,* 16, 74–113.

Mika, K. L., and Kluger, M. P. (October 19, 1990). *Respondent anonymity vs. confidentiality: Differences in results of an internal agency survey.* Paper presented at the Annual Conference of the American Evaluation Association, Washington, DC.

Nunnally, J. C. (1978). *Psychometric Theory* (2nd ed.). New York: McGraw-Hill.

Peterson, R. A. (1988). *Marketing Research* (2nd ed.). Plano, TX: Business Publications.

Reichers, A. E., & Schneider, B. (1990). Climate and culture: An evolution of constructs. In B. Schneider (Ed.), *Organizational climate and culture* (pp. 4-39). San Francisco: Jossey-Bass.

Schneider, B., Parkington, J. J., & Buxton, V. M. (1980). Employee and customer perceptions of service in banks. *Administrative Science Quarterly*, 25, 252–267.

Sudman, S. (1976). *Applied sampling*. New York: Academic Press.

6

Assessing Image and Community Awareness

Large for-profit organizations actively pursue an understanding of the public's awareness of, and attitudes and behaviors toward, their products and services. Marketing, selling, and profit-making depend on how the service or product is viewed at a given time.

Nonprofit organizations should also be interested in the public's awareness and perceptions of them and their services. A simple community awareness study will answer basic questions. How many residents have heard of the organization? To what degree do they know specific details about the organization, such as the type of services it provides and whether it is a public or private organization, for-profit or nonprofit?

Awareness and image—that is, how the organization is perceived or characterized—affect both those trying to access services and those considering charitable donations. Before the organization can serve the community, and before it can be the beneficiary of a charitable donation, people must first be aware of its existence. Then they must be aware of its mission, services, and location, and of their eligibility for receipt of its services.

For example, are the services of an organization with a religious affiliation in its title available to people of all denominations? Is the organization part of the state government or a private organization? Is one asked to pay high fees for services, is there a sliding fee scale based on the client's ability to pay, or is there a means test?

Once awareness of the organization's existence and services has been assessed, one may want to know the most salient characteristics or attributes identified with the organization. Key constituents, such as community residents, those referring clients to the organization, and staff members, are possible candidates for providing this information. Those who set strategic direction for the organization, such as board members, may also be included. Volunteers for the organization, donors to the organization, and the organization's clients are other important constituents who may be asked for their views.

This information can be useful in developing or publicizing services, as well as in correcting misperceptions among those who think they know the organization, such as staff members, board members, volunteers, and referring sources. Perhaps it is most important to make sure that misperceptions are not creating barriers to clients' access to services. Are potential clients not approaching the organization because of a mistaken belief that services are expensive, only open to those of a particular religion, or not available from the organization?

Conducting the Study

Once the purpose of the study has been decided by those commissioning the collection of information, as well as any other interested parties, participants must be selected. Who will answer the questions? Are the questions appropriate for all targeted audiences, or are different questions to be asked of each group?

The way in which the information is to be collected must be determined next. Responses on awareness of the organization and on its image may be gathered separately or together. A simple community awareness study answers basic questions about how many residents have heard of the organization and what they know about it, such as the services offered and locations. An image study examines how the organization is viewed by key constituents. In either case, several issues must be considered.

Focusing the Questions

The information sought dictates the questions asked. If the study is to assess whether people have heard of the organization, participants will be asked to name any organizations in the area that provide particular services. For example, can the participant name any adoption agencies in the area? This kind of question solicits awareness on an unaided basis, that is, recall of the organization's name using an open-ended question, without any hints. If the goal is to find out whether people are aware of a specific type of adoption service offered by the organization, participants may be asked whether they know, for example, the names of any organizations involved in international adoption.

Awareness may be assessed on an aided basis by asking study participants whether they have heard of the organization after being told its name. For example, the participants may be asked if they knew that agency XYZ offered adoption services.

Selecting Participants

To select participants, one must return to the purpose of the study. If the sponsor of the study wants to know whether community residents are aware of the organization, then residents must be included in the study. If the sponsor wants to know what aspects of the organization charitable contributors particularly like, then previous donors ought to be included in the study. Current clients are another possibility, as are staff members and members of the board of directors. Past and present volunteers are yet another potential group to examine. For future recruiting purposes, it might be helpful to know what in particular made them want to volunteer.

Collecting Information

One popular way of gathering information, particularly from a group not associated with the organization, is through telephone interviews. An advantage of this format is that participants can be asked to recall the organization's name first on an unaided basis and then on an aided basis. A mailed survey is another way, offering the advantages of wide distribution, inclusion of those without telephones, and low data collection time and expense. Its disadvantages include low return rates, frequently as low as 30% [Stropher and Meyburg 1979]; participation percentages will usually be higher for a telephone survey [Communication Briefings 1988]. Mailed surveys are unsuitable for some purposes—for example, for asking an unaided question followed by an aided question on awareness of the organization. Although one may ask, on an aided basis, whether participants have heard of the organization, it would be impossible to ask them to name an organization on an unaided basis in the same survey.

Focus groups offer yet another way to obtain information about awareness and image. Using the nominal group technique described in chapter 3, participants representative of the population under study may be asked to identify key attributes of the organization or of a particular service. The answers may then form the basis of questions asked in a telephone interview or survey.

Care should be taken to keep the interview or survey as brief as possible. For a telephone conversation with a stranger, three to five minutes may be the most time that can be expected. To determine how long an interview will take, it can be tried out and timed; this also helps to sharpen the questions until they are so clear, concise, and to the point that they elicit quick responses.

Bilingual Accommodation

It is important to take into account the languages spoken in a given population. Every resident called, including non-English-speaking residents, must have an equal opportunity to contribute if the findings are to apply to the whole population under investigation. Written surveys should be available in translation for non-English speaking participants.

Sample Bias

For at least three reasons, it is important to be sure the sample does not differ significantly from the total population from which it was drawn.

1. The findings can then be generalized with confidence to the larger group of interest.
2. Comparing demographic information (age, income, gender, race/ethnicity, marital status, occupation, length of residence in the community, number of children in the household) provides some assurance that participants were randomly selected.
3. If not everyone contacted agrees to participate, it is possible to determine whether those who refused did so in a selective way, resulting in a sample that may not represent the original population.

The Experience of the Village for Families and Children

Community Awareness Study

Several years ago, the authors' organization, known at the time by another name, undertook a community awareness survey. The agency has been in existence for more than 180 years and has undergone many changes. Understandable confusion existed in the community about the types of services the agency currently offered, its affiliations, and its location. The study was requested by the agency's director of communications, public relations, and resource development, who wanted to know whether local residents had heard of the agency and whether they distinguished it from other organizations with similar sounding names. This information would then be used in preparing pamphlets, press releases, and other materials publicizing individual services and the agency overall, as well as in developing fund-raising strategies.

The study questions sought to determine the percentage of local residents who could recall the agency's name on an unaided basis and then on an aided basis. The participants were first asked to name any of the social service agencies in the Greater Hartford area. A definition of social service agency was included when requested.

If the agency's name was not mentioned in response to this question, participants were told the agency's name and that it provides mental health services and social services of all kinds to children and families. They were then asked if they had heard of the agency. Further questions were asked of those who responded in the affirmative, while only demographic information was obtained from the remainder.

The additional questions for those responding affirmatively related to areas where the director thought there might be some confusion: whether they thought the organization was a private or a state agency; whether they knew of the agency by any other names; and how they had learned of the agency, with possible responses including radio, newspaper, telephone yellow pages, have seen the sign, and friend or relative.

Participants were also asked where the agency was located, and responses were scored as correct or incorrect. If incorrect, the participant was told the correct location. A correct response lent credence to the earlier answer that he or she was aware of the agency. Participants were asked what they knew about the agency, and what specific services the agency offered. If participants seemed interested in knowing, the interviewer told them of other services that were not mentioned in their response.

The remaining questions elicited information on demographic characteristics of those responding to the survey and other factors thought to be associated with awareness of the agency. Questions were asked about

- length of time the participant had lived in the Greater Hartford area,
- number of children living in the household,
- gender and marital status,

- age,
- race/ethnicity, and
- income.

How Information Was Collected

The vehicle for collecting this information was a brief telephone survey of area residents. The sample was randomly selected from the white pages of the telephone book, targeting the exchanges of the five residential areas nearest the agency.

As a public service, market research students at a local university volunteered to be interviewers, and about 50 students received training in telephone interviewing techniques. Several who were fluent in Spanish were available to interview residents who only spoke Spanish.

The interview script was tested and the time reduced to approximately three minutes. Most of the calls had to be made in the evening between 5 PM and 9 PM. The questions were asked of any family member 18 years of age or older. Of the 543 individuals telephoned, 226, or 42%, were reached and agreed to participate in the study.

Findings

The results were tabulated by the agency's research and evaluation department. In general, unaided awareness of the agency was a low 7%. This figure, however, must be placed in the context of the fact that no other social service agency named received a higher percentage. When prompted with the agency's name, the percentage of awareness increased to 53%.

Those who said they were aware of the organization were most likely to have heard of it through newspapers. When probed further, however, half thought that the organization was a government agency, and may actually have been recalling newspaper articles about the state child welfare agency. This interpretation was further supported by the incorrect address often given when asked about the agency's location.

Various demographic characteristics were examined in relation to awareness. Although women were more likely than men to have heard of the agency, all other factors were unrelated, including the number of years living in the area, age, marital status, race/ethnicity, and income.

The findings were interpreted with caution because minorities and poor persons in the local area made up a smaller percentage of the sample than would have been anticipated on the basis of census information for the Greater Hartford Community.

Image Study

Partly in response to the community awareness study's finding on the lack of distinctiveness and confusion about the agency and its name, a board task force was formed to more carefully examine the organization's image. The task force commissioned the agency's research and evaluation department to identify and rank-order those characteristics and attributes that were important to the agency's key constituents. In addition to providing detailed information for use in fund-raising, brochures, and other publicity, the study could also help the agency decide whether or not to change its name.

The items for this survey were based on the agency's mission statement and associated goals developed by the organization's top management group, and also included questions about the agency's identity as a private nonprofit. Groups familiar with the agency (see below) were asked how strongly they agreed with statements about the agency, and whether they saw the agency as

- innovative and flexible,
- committed to helping children,
- notable for the excellence of its service programs, and
- an established agency with a heritage of consistent service to the community.

Participants familiar with the agency were then asked to rate how important each of these characteristics would be to the agency's clients. For example, while the organization may be known as an established agency with a heritage of consistent service to the community, this characteristic may rank low in importance for agency clients. Participants were also given the opportunity to add any characteristics of the agency that had not already been mentioned in the interview.

Participants unfamiliar with the agency (potential donors) were asked to rate how important a set of statements and traits would be in forming an opinion about the value of services offered by a human services agency. The statements were the same as those rated by the participants familiar with the agency. This second group was also given the opportunity to describe any additional characteristics they considered especially important in deciding whether to support a human services agency.

How Information Was Collected

The board's task force was interested in the perceptions of five groups: staff members, board members, agency volunteers, current agency funders, and potential donors. A telephone interview format was selected and tested to reduce the interview time and clear up any confusion about the wording of questions.

The characteristics or traits were rated using a six-point scale that ranged from strongly agree to strongly disagree, or very important to not at all important, depending on the question. Participants other than the potential donor group received a letter from the chair of the task force alerting them to the upcoming interview.

The agency's two research assistants conducted all the interviews. The interviews with those familiar with the agency took about five to ten minutes to complete; the interviews with potential donors lasted approximately five minutes. A total of 168 people completed the telephone interview. Nearly all the staff members, board members, volunteers, and funders contacted participated in the study. Only about one-third of the potential donors contacted, however, agreed to be interviewed; findings from this group must be interpreted with caution.

Findings

Based on the six-point scales, an arithmetic average was calculated for each statement. The average statement ratings were rank-ordered from highest agreement (or importance) ratings to lowest agreement (or importance) ratings. The rankings from the various constituent groups were compared with one another. The characteristics that had the greatest consensus among key constituents as describing the agency and as important to clients and potential donors were

- committed to or known for helping children,
- committed to families or family members at risk, and
- notable for the excellence of its professional staff.

Unlike the staff members, board members, and volunteers, the potential donors significantly underrated the importance of being a private, nonprofit agency.

This information about the agency's image as perceived by its key constituents was useful during deliberations around changing the agency's name to "The Village for Families and Children, Inc.," and will be helpful in future publicity.

References

Communication Briefings. (1988). *Mastering marketing: Helping you and your employees succeed in marketing your organization.* Pitman, NJ: Communication Publications and Resources.

Stropher, P. R., & Meyburg, A. H. (1979). *Survey sampling and multivariate analysis for social scientists and engineers.* Lexington, MA: D C Heath.

P lanning for Downsizing

7

Nonprofit organizations, like those in the for-profit sector, have struggled financially during these difficult economic times. Many are faced with increasing costs for health care and salaries and decreasing support from traditional funding sources, such as the government and United Way [Koteen 1989]. Competition is also developing from other nonprofit organizations, as well as for-profit organizations encroaching on what has traditionally been considered the sole domain of the nonprofit organization. Further, many nonprofit organizations are serving clients who are either poor, or near poor and therefore ineligible for government assistance programs. The small portion of service costs that clients may have paid in the past is swiftly eroding.

The nonprofit organization must struggle to survive in this difficult economic climate. The recent personal experience of the authors and the lessons learned provide the basis for these suggestions on how to proceed if downsizing becomes necessary.

The Need to Be Proactive and Anticipatory

An organization faced with difficult times must deal with the situation proactively. The first step is to assess the current and future situation. Any bad news that can be anticipated, such as funding cutbacks and increased expenses, can also be planned for. Managing the current year in an anticipatory manner is the first step in planning for the future. It is essential to avoid a crisis mode, where quick decisions are made without taking the time to consider options carefully and prepare the organization.

85

Planning must take place when revenue shortfalls are first anticipated. Developing contingency budget management strategies is the
place to begin. Contingency planning is used to deal with uncertainty,
trouble that may, or may not, happen [Friend and Hickling 1987].
When framing contingency plans, it is important to anticipate the
worst possible revenue shortfalls as well as any unforeseen expenses.

If the executive director or CEO does not already make a practice
of periodically advising staff members of conditions that may positive-
ly or negatively affect the organization, now is the time to start.
Nonprofit organizations are, by definition, required to fulfill missions
that center on helping others who are unable to help themselves.
Staff members often see the delivery of services as the most important
element, however, and view the economics that affect revenues available to carry out the mission as management's responsibility.
Consequently, nonprofit organization staff members are not likely to
be oriented to market forces and competition. Even contingency budgets, however, cannot be developed meaningfully without being
connected to those external dynamics. The CEO and other key managers must help the entire staff understand market forces and
competition and connect them to the organization's management of
its services.

Hearing about external issues, and engaging in dialogue about
their effect on the organization, prepares staff members for upcoming budget decisions that may reduce benefits and services and
consequently staff size, disrupting workplace security. In a professional organization, budget cuts are perceived as threats to professional
standards, quality, and creativity. This viewpoint cannot be ignored.

Understanding financial matters as they affect service delivery
provides a common template for managing and planning. Second, it
stimulates staff members to find ways to deliver services more efficiently and to uncover new revenue streams. Awareness of
marketplace forces also enables staff members to be conscious of con-
trolling service costs to remain competitive.

Contingency Planning

In anticipation of current-year budget shortfalls, top management
must develop strategies to keep fiscal outcomes in balance. Contingency planning is a process that formulates strategies for midstream
adjustments to existing budgets. There are many approaches to contingency planning.

Directing managers to reduce expenses incrementally across the organization is a common and often-used strategy. This strategy entails selecting a percentage that will be used as a guide for expense reduction throughout the organization. It is based on the presumption that all budgets can be reduced by the given percentage with reasonably even impact. It assumes that no part of the organization would be materially undermined in its ability to provide reliable services either to clients or to the organization.

The authors believe, however, that this is not a valid assumption in any organization, and that across-the-board, incremental expense reduction is the least strategic option available—one that is not likely to serve the short- or long-term needs of the organization. Even the contingency budget planning process should be strategic and directional. It should include a risk assessment and an evaluation of the marketplace condition of each service, program, or function.

Each revenue stream should be rated as safe, moderately at risk, or at high risk. Safe revenues are those for which funding commitments are not affected at all by external trends or the volume of service. Moderate-risk revenues are predominantly, but not fully, funded by commitments that are unaffected by external trends or the volume of service. High-risk revenues, however, are those predominantly connected with the volume of service delivered, at a time when primary purchasers of the service, such as clients and third-party customers, are vulnerable to loss of revenue or have altered their funding priorities.

Special attention should be given to those programs or services that are found to be highly vulnerable to poor economic conditions. Those rated at high or moderate risk require a plan that can make adjustments to expenses for the remainder of the budget period. As part of the contingency planning, impact statements should be prepared to describe what effect expense reductions will have on the quantity and quality of service, on clients, on the work force, and on the organization's strategic goals.

In a volatile funding environment, every service should have a contingency plan, but this is especially important for services with income sources at high or moderate risk. When income sources are so rated, it is a reflection on market forces as they bear on a particular service. The plans developed should identify specific revenue enhancements or expense reductions to be made by a particular date. The plans should be further supported by hard commitments for funding, trend analyses, and cash-flow projections. New income sources might include

- Increasing billable units of service without increasing corresponding expenses;
- Increasing prices, depending on what the market will bear; and
- Redirecting ways that a service is delivered to achieve a greater return on investment, such as reallocating staff member time to activities that generate revenue.

Expense reductions might include

- Filling vacant positions with entry-level candidates, who command lower salaries than more experienced persons;
- Not filling vacancies, or systematically delaying filling vacancies;
- Modifying staffing patterns to achieve needed services without retaining the same level of staffing costs;
- Reducing supply expenses and photocopying costs; and
- Reducing organizational memberships in professional associations.

Care must be taken to select tactics for revenue enhancement or expense reduction that lend themselves to timely implementation. Contingency planning is not typically a process that allows for a let's-wait-and-see approach, or for subsequent planning and analysis. Plans must be available for implementation when problems emerge. It is helpful to predefine the conditions that will signal plan implementation. Careful monitoring should begin immediately for services with revenues considered at high risk.

Budget Planning

In this section, the term *budget planning* refers to the process that is typically used to craft a program and financial plan for a new fiscal period. It is more future oriented than contingency planning, but has to include much of the thinking described in contingency planning. Particular attention is given to budget planning in a climate that calls for a conscious, yet coherent plan for shrinking the organization to bring it into alignment with market forces. It is planning that has a high probability for staffing reductions, because so much of the nonprofit organization's budget is devoted to the personnel who deliver human services.

Roles and Responsibilities

How the organization's leaders carry out their roles, from the start of planning to the finish, will influence how easy or difficult it will be to implement the final plan. Four major planning roles are involved in this process.

Executive Director/Chief Executive Officer

The chief executive officer of the organization sets the stage for planning. Preparatory communication should begin with informing the board of directors (or other governing body of the nonprofit organization) of emerging threats, challenges, and opportunities. It is helpful if the executive has made a point of periodically advising the board and staff of changing conditions that will affect the agency. Whether or not staff members have been prepared for such a presentation, they must now hear from the executive about those events and conditions that will influence the budget planning process. At a time like this, a meeting or series of meetings provides much more effective communication and interchange than could be achieved by a memo. In a meeting, the executive director can anticipate problematic reactions, receive and answer questions, and generally promote universal and accurate understanding on the part of staff members. He or she can

- Acknowledge the anxiety that everyone feels under these conditions, including the difficulty of tolerating inevitable ambiguities and uncertainties, and the importance of communication to manage this anxiety;
- Describe the changes in the external environment that will adversely affect the organization;
- Establish an awareness among staff members of growing competition and the need to price services competitively;
- Involve staff members by inviting their ideas and suggestions;
- Encourage staff members to develop creative ways to deliver services with fewer dollars;
- Encourage staff members to uncover new revenue streams;
- Prepare staff members for decisions that would reduce expenses associated with benefits, salaries, or other important staff member supports; and
- Emphasize the importance of developing tolerance for change as the external community shifts its interests and priorities, thereby reducing predictability.

It is especially important for the executive director to orient managers to the downsizing task. They must see that this difficult task is not a result of failure to lead the organization effectively, but rather an understandable outcome of environmental conditions. They must also understand and believe that a period of realignment can reposition the agency for the future. If the planning job is done well and is linked to a sound strategic plan, the planning should position the agency to capitalize on changing opportunities.

As options for downsizing unfold, the executive director should attend divisional or service meetings to discuss this information in small group settings. The authors have found that it helps to invite staff members to offer opinions and suggestions about organizationwide options. Changes that affect everyone, like production expectations, hours, and suppressing raises or time off, can be discussed with all staff members. In fact, it is helpful to solicit their opinions on such options. Knowing where there is support for expense reductions can be extremely valuable when decisions are made and interpreted.

The authors do not recommend, however, involving staff members in public discussions about what services or products should be preserved or reduced. That would engage them in decisions that could affect the jobs of their peers, and place them in significant competition and conflict. The executive should encourage staff members who have additional suggestions or questions after meetings to contact him or her directly. Employees appreciate knowledge, rather than secrecy, even in the face of unpleasant news.

Top Management

At the request of the executive director, top managers will develop a downsized budget plan that represents a number of uncomfortable decisions. They will engage in a critical analysis of the areas they manage and of the organization as a whole. This is a process loaded with potential intra-leadership conflict, as they will be

- assessing the risks of revenue streams,
- identifying new income sources,
- deciding on expense reductions among services,
- shaping organizationwide expense reductions, and
- making decisions about what services or products will remain, and in what state.

Retreats are helpful for brainstorming ideas and reviewing suggestions from all viewpoints. These top management retreats can also reaffirm commonly held visions for the organization and generate group support for the difficult planning and decisions ahead. There is a greater chance for consensus when the self-oriented needs and concerns of individuals in the group are eased and they can focus on problems in a pleasant atmosphere [Collins and Guetzkow 1964].

Key management also has a responsibility for communicating with middle management, soliciting their ideas, and involving them in the budget planning. To be sure that all the information needed has been given, all income or expense projections should be reviewed by top and middle management.

Middle Management/Service Directors

Middle managers participate in the planning for downsizing particularly as it relates to their services. When options directly affect their program and their staff, they must be involved at the earliest possible time. Agencywide options generated by top managers should be reviewed, and opportunity provided to react to these ideas. In the early stages of planning, they should also be encouraged to add options to the list.

Middle managers have an important responsibility to help the organization through the downsizing planning period. They will need to convey information to other staff members, who are understandably anxious during this process. Middle managers must also be the conduit for suggestions and concerns their staff members raise. With the assistance of top management, middle managers may anticipate staff reactions to downsizing. These reactions include

- intellectual understanding but emotional distress, including anger;
- heightened competition between services of the organization;
- a perception that management expects more for less;
- objections to the organization undertaking new initiatives;
- increased resistance to change in general;
- talk of turnover;
- a magnification of minor day-to-day problems; and
- a decline in efficiency due to anxiety about downsizing.

Middle management must develop ways to handle these reactions, including discussing matters openly, showing care and concern, and conveying that these difficult decisions are necessary to position the organization for a brighter future.

Staff Members

The input of staff members can be successfully sought on budget options that affect the entire organization. Some of these options include

- deferring salary increases;
- instituting different salary increases for different job categories, as determined by turnover rates and the ease or difficulty of filling such positions;
- increasing the workweek;
- decreasing the workweek;
- increasing the staff member's share of health insurance costs;
- freezing vacancies;
- freezing promotions;
- canceling bonuses and recognition and/or incentive awards;
- reducing or canceling training for staff members; and
- reducing or canceling travel allocations for staff members.

The options can be presented with information about the financial impact of each one on the organization. Exposing problems and involving all staff members in the downsizing process heightens anxiety. It also, however, offers everyone a chance to know the options under consideration and to participate by sharing their views. While they need not hear all the specifics, they should be given an explanation of the process being used to evaluate services. The more that staff members feel they have been involved, the more ready they will be to support the final decisions.

Each staff member has a role in assuring that the decisions made regarding downsizing are the best ones possible. How they manage themselves during these tense times, including their discussions within the greater community, can have a significant impact on the organization's position in the community, so staff members should understand these dynamics.

Preparing and Engaging the Board of Directors

The board of directors of the nonprofit organization will make the final decision to approve or reject a plan for downsizing. Top management should do everything possible to prepare the board for receipt of such a proposal. Management must also prepare a proposal that can be approved by the board of directors. Exchanges of information must take place during the planning process. There are several ways to prepare a board of directors and engage them in planning.

Briefing on External Events Affecting the Organization

As described earlier, the CEO informs the board of directors or other governing body of the nonprofit organization of the difficulties occurring, or anticipated, in the near future. Being aware of these difficulties prepares them to understand the context for a proposed downsizing plan.

Relationship to Mission

The board of directors is responsible for setting the mission of the nonprofit organization and assuring that the organization abides by it. In relation to downsizing, therefore, the board will test how each proposed reduction relates to the organization's mission. Top management would be well advised to have this information ready, both orally and in written form.

Relationship to Strategic Plan

The board of directors also is responsible for setting strategic direction for the organization's future. Progress on fulfilling the strategic plan is expected and monitored by the board. The strategic plan and its priorities then, must be thoughtfully and carefully considered when downsizing the organization. As with the organization's mission, top management should be prepared to document this consideration and its influence in the development of the downsizing plan. Management should also be prepared to discuss and answer any questions at board meetings about the relationship between the strategic plan and the downsizing proposal. The board of directors adopts strategic priorities with the intention that these priorities will influence the organization's direction, and expects progress regardless of economic conditions or commitments to traditional endeavors.

Progress Reports

The organization's top executive may meet individually with key board members, such as the chairs of the board's executive committee and strategic planning and evaluation committees, to orient them to the planning process. It is crucial for them to understand that top management is leading an effort that includes full consideration of existing board policy. These meetings also offer an opportunity to reemphasize the delicate balance between the mission and the strategic plan, on one hand, and a difficult financial position, on the other.

The board's executive committee may be presented with the range of downsizing options currently under consideration. Top management and board members have the opportunity to discuss the relative values of the different options. Management can then see the areas of agreement and difference and can incorporate this knowledge into the development and presentation of recommendations.

References

Collins, B., & Guetzkow, H. A. (1964). *A social psychology of group process for decision making.* New York: Wiley.

Friend, J., & Hickling, A. (1987). *Planning under pressure: The strategic choice approach.* Elmsford, NY: Pergamon Press, Inc.

Koteen, J. (1989). *Strategic management in public and nonprofit organizations.* New York: Praeger.

8

Tools for Downsizing

Once all the suggestions for increasing revenues and decreasing expenses have been generated, it is useful to have a format with which to organize this material. Some of the options for cutting expenses would be implemented across the entire organization, such as reducing the stipends available for staff member training. Other options might be specific to a service or division.

It is helpful to divide the suggestions on paper into those that affect staff members across the organization and those that are service- or division-specific. Beside each option should be an estimate of the savings that would be gained by carrying it out.

The savings may be further organized into operating and capital expenses, the former pertaining to the day-to-day running of the organization and the latter to buildings and grounds, bricks and mortar. Service-related options should be distinguished from administrative options. Service-related options might include reductions in the staff training program and in the staffing of particular services, as well as reductions via reorganization of top management. Administrative options could include reductions in the incentive pay pool and in vacation time and increases in the length of the workweek.

Revenue-generating strategies may also be divided into organizationwide strategies versus strategies specific to a service or division. Beside each income-generating proposal should be a conservative estimate of the amount of money that would be produced if it were carried out.

Planning Grid for Line Functions

A tool developed by the Village for Families and Children may be useful to other nonprofit organizations undergoing downsizing. This tool, referred to as the planning grid for line functions, helps assess the contribution of each of the organization's services (see figure 1). It provides a method or discipline for ranking the relative worth of each of the organization's service or products, thereby providing guidance to reduction and retention decisions. This exercise also documents a careful and thoughtful budget-making process. It may well be presented to the overseeing body, such as the board of directors, during the budgeting period. Further, the planning grid is a way to encourage communication and involve staff members in examining the issues. The grid lends objectivity, reducing the emotionalism that often crops up during the budgeting process.

The planning grid is divided into five sections with categories in each section. Each category has a five-point rating scale:

> 5 = high
> 4 = medium high
> 3 = medium
> 2 = medium low
> 1 = low

The sum score of the category ratings may be used to rank the services of the organization. The greater the total score, the higher the relative ranking of that service. If not all categories are applicable, then average scores may be computed and rank-ordered.

Section 1: Strategic Priority/Mission Issues

The categories in this first section of the planning grid have to do with the organization's strategic priorities and mission. There are more categories in this section than in some of the others, and because the overall service rating is found by totaling the category scores, more weight is given to this section. This is intentional, because the innovative organization is serious about strategic planning. One category in this section, for example, gives points only to those services that have made real progress on strategic plans.

Categories

Strategic priority/primary problem percentage. What percentage of cases or clients have a primary problem in one of the organization's strategic

97

Ratings: Five point scale where 5 = high 1 = low

Division / Service	Strategic priority/mission issues					Financial issues					Value considerations			Marketing considerations			Impact of eliminating function					Total	Average
	Strategic priority/primary problem percentage	Congruence with mission	Progress on strategic plans	Urban/low-income clients	Contribution to future position	Ability to compete on cost	Budget performance	Income growth potential	Current level of endowment support	Endowment dependency	Documented effectiveness	Innovation	Internal collaboration	Other providers	Number of interested funders	Demand for service	Current level of endowment support	Strategic priority/primary problem percentage	Staff impact	Client impact	Community impact		

Figure 1. Planning Grid for Line Functions

priority areas? A high rating might be given to services with 100% of their cases or clients in the priority areas; a medium rating to services with at least two-thirds of their cases in the priority areas; and a low rating to services with less than two-thirds of their cases in the priority areas. These cutoffs were based on previous information about the organization, which showed that services divided roughly into one-third high, one-third medium, and one-third low scores when they were rated on this scale.

Congruence with mission. To what degree does a service entail the points or components of the organization's mission? If there is a written mission statement, each element of the mission may be extracted and each service rated on how completely it addresses the elements. A high rating would be given to services that encompass all points in the organization's mission statement, and a medium or low rating to services that do not completely address all points. Note that the ratings of medium and low are relative, and based on the actual range of possible scores for the organization. For example, it is unlikely that an organization has any service completely unrelated to its mission. The organization's lowest-rated service might still meet half the points in the mission statement.

Progress on strategic plans. To what degree has a service progressed on its strategic priorities? Progress may be assessed in several ways, including

- related training offered to staff members,
- increased percentage of clients with primary problems or reasons for accessing the service that are related to the organization's strategic priorities, and
- progress on specific efforts tied to delivering the service in a way that addresses the strategic priorities.

A high rating might be given to services that have made marked progress in at least two of the three areas just outlined. Depending on the organization and whether any service of the organization could receive this rating, the highest mark might be given only to those services that had offered training, increased the percentage of clients, and made progress on specific strategic priority-related efforts. If that is a realistic standard, then a medium rating might be given to a service that had made marked progress in two of the three areas, and a low rating to a service with little or no progress.

Urban/low-income clients. What are the demographic characteristics of the population a service has targeted for receipt of treatment or services? For example, if a service is intended for urban and low-income clients, then it can be rated on whether an acceptable proportion of clients seen actually fit that description. A high rating can be given to services that fully meet the target of clients to be provided for. A medium rating might be given to services whose recipients match a portion of the demographic characteristics targeted, and a low rating to services that are not serving the population targeted for service by the organization.

Contribution to future position. To what degree have significant community needs or trends been anticipated and addressed by the service? Documented efforts may be assessed, and a high rating given to services well positioned to meet the future needs of current and potential clients. Guidelines for medium and low ratings would be determined by specifics of the organization.

Section 2: Financial Issues

The second section on the planning grid also contains five categories, thereby giving a significant weighting to financial considerations. The categories in this section include the service's budget performance and income-growth potential. While it may be the mission of a nonprofit organization to serve clients regardless of their ability to pay, it would be impossible to serve any clients if the organization did not act in a fiscally responsible manner. Many nonprofit organizations are increasingly concerned with the bottom line as income sources shrink and expenses grow. Additionally, some nonprofit organizations offer a variety of services, some of which must be subsidized by income from other more profitable services. Service to clients regardless of ability to pay and fiscal responsibility must be delicately balanced, if the nonprofit organization is to remain a viable and valued entity.

Categories

Ability to compete on cost. In a competitive climate, the organization seeks to sell its services to a variety of customers. These customers may be the state or municipality, a federated fund-raising organization, third-party insurance carriers, or service recipients. In every case the price is going to be evaluated against what others charge for the same or like services. If the organization's cost to deliver the service drives its price well above the competition, it will be increasingly difficult to find a market. Depending on the organization, a high rating might be given to services with fees that exceed actual costs (turn a profit). A medium rating might be given to services with fees that balance costs, and a low rating to services with fees that are below cost (that operate at a loss).

Budget performance. To what extent has the service demonstrated its ability to control financial performance over time? Again depending on what makes sense for the organization, a high rating might be given to services with budget surpluses of 3% or greater for at least two consecutive years. A medium rating could be given to services that had deficits not larger than 5%, for example, and showed an improvement from the previous year. A low rating might then be given to services with consecutive annual deficits larger than 5%.

Income growth potential. To what degree does a service have real and imminent opportunities for new income, rather than solely hoped-for results? A high rating may be given to services that have already shown growth and see more opportunities in the future. A medium rating could be given in instances where some opportunities for income growth appear, although nothing has yet materialized, and a low rating where no opportunities are currently available or seem likely for the future.

Current level of endowment support. For some nonprofit organizations, an endowment funds part of the operating expenses. The endowment may make up the shortfall after external income sources are used to fund service expenditures. For those organizations with endowment income, the portion of endowment each service receives can be assessed. A high rating could be given to services that do not require much endowment support, and a low rating to services requiring significant endowment support.

Endowment dependency. For organizations with an endowment, services might also be rated on the percentage of the service budget that is supported by endowment dollars. A high rating, for example, could be given to services with endowment support of less than 10%, a medium rating to services with 10% to 20% endowment support, and a low rating to services with endowment dollars exceeding 20% of the service's budget.

Section 3: Value Considerations

In assessing the contribution of a service to the organization, factors important to the values or culture of an organization may be included. Because the diversity of services offered is seen as a strength, to be used to the client's greatest advantage, one category might reward collaboration across services of the organization. Organizations that value offering excellent services to clients may include a category on the documented effectiveness of services. Innovation, an underpinning of strategic planning, may be another category for organizations that value and encourage creativity and new ventures as a reflection of the changing needs of the clients served.

Categories

Documented effectiveness. Do positive outcomes occur for the clients receiving the service, and have these outcomes been documented? Positive results may be documented in formal outcome effectiveness studies, client satisfaction surveys, or other evaluations done recently, perhaps within the past three years. A high rating may be given to services with three or more indicators (studies) documenting their effectiveness. A medium rating could be given to services with one or two indicators, and a low rating to services with no documentation of effectiveness. It is important to be stringent in deciding what is an acceptable form of documentation, being careful to avoid hearsay and other soft sources of information.

Innovation. To what extent is a service new, creative, or venturesome? Was this effort part of the organization five years ago? A high rating might be given to services that are new or have done something new, creative, or venturesome within the past few years. A medium rating could correspond to some modest changes in these areas, and a low rating might indicate a stagnant service.

Internal collaboration. To what extent have joint efforts been undertaken between this service and other services in the organization? Joint efforts may be measured in two ways: collaboration across services on projects or programs, and ease of referring clients from one service to another within the organization. A high rating could be earned when both types of collaboration are present, a medium rating when one type of collaboration is present, and a low rating when no collaboration is seen between one service and another.

Section 4: Marketing Considerations

The categories in this section rate the demand for services, the availability of similar services from other sources, and the number and variety of funding sources.

Categories

Other providers. Are other individuals or organizations providing essentially the same service? A high rating could be given to services with

one or no competitors, a medium rating to services with a few competitors, and a low rating to services with many competitors. The
definitions of *few* and *many* may be determined by the particular
organization.

Number of interested funders. How many individuals and/or organizations are willing to fund the service? Are they all from one type
of funding source, such as the government or private sector, or are
they from a mix of sources? A high rating might be given to services
with either multiple types of funding sources or several funders
from one type of source, such as several grantors. Medium and low
ratings could be given in proportion to number and diversity of
funding sources.

Demand for service. What has the trend been over time with regard
to demand for the service? A high rating might be given to services
where demand is growing by at least 5% per year, for example. A medium rating could be given to services with a steady, neither decreasing
nor increasing, demand for service, and a low rating to services where
demand has declined by at least 5% per year. The cutoff points selected
should make sense in terms of this organization's services, and may be
higher or lower than the 5% measure used in this example.

Section 5: Impact of Eliminating Function

Because one of the uses of this tool is to select what service to eliminate, if such a decision becomes necessary, a fifth section is included.
Notice that it repeats one earlier category from the Strategic Priority
section and one from Financial Issues, adding extra weight to these
categories that appear twice in the grid. This section also examines
the impact on staff members, clients, and the community if a service
were to be eliminated.

Categories

Current level of endowment support. As described earlier, for those organizations with endowment income, the portion of endowment received
by a service can be assessed. High ratings, which favor retention, could
be given to services receiving little or no endowment, while medium
and low ratings might be given in proportion to the percentage of the
organization's endowment distributed to the service.

Strategic priority/primary problem percentage. Again, this category assesses the percentage of cases or clients whose primary problem is in one
of the organization's strategic priority areas. A high rating, which favors
retention, might be given to services with 100% of their cases or clients

in the priority areas. Medium and low ratings would correspond to decreasing percentages of clients with problems in the priority areas.

Staff impact. To what extent will the organization's employees be affected if the service is eliminated? Ratings will depend on the number of staff members employed in the service and how easy it would be to redirect them to other jobs within the organization. A high rating, which favors retention, might be given to services where more than 10 staff members would be affected, with most of those affected not able to transfer to another position in the organization. A medium rating might be given to services whose elimination would affect five to 10 staff members, and a low rating to services whose elimination would affect less than five staff members. These staff member ranges should be based on the typical size of a service within the organization, and increased or decreased accordingly.

Client impact. To what degree would clients be affected if a service were eliminated? Are there other places these clients could go to receive the same service? A high rating, which favors retention, might be given to a service if more than 75% of its clients would not be able to receive similar services elsewhere. A medium rating could be given to a service if 25% to 75% of its clients would not be able to receive similar services elsewhere, and a low rating might be given when fewer than 25% of clients would not be able to receive similar services elsewhere.

Community impact. To what extent would elimination of a particular service adversely affect the organization's image in the community, including reputation, visibility, and relationships with other key local organizations? A high rating, which favors retention, might be given when service elimination would have a significantly negative impact on the organization's image in the community. Medium and low ratings could reflect less impact and no impact on community perception of the agency should the service be eliminated.

Planning Grid for Support Functions

Comprehensive planning includes an examination of administrative support activities, denoted as support functions, as well as services, considered line functions and treated in the previous grid. Examples of these support functions are

- accounting,
- food services,
- human resources,

- information services,
- maintenance,
- communications/public relations,
- development, and
- research and evaluation.

Both board members and staff members should know that support functions will receive the same critical assessment as line functions. Although nonprofit organizations cannot meet licensing and accreditation requirements without a competent administrative infrastructure, that does not argue for excluding essential support functions from critical evaluation. A planning grid (see figure 2) can be applied just as meaningfully to support functions as to line functions.

By applying the same ranking method or discipline as that for the line functions, consensus can be generated on a decision to modify support functions or contract for them externally. High scores and rankings favor retention of a function, while lower scores suggest eliminating it and contracting externally. Although some of the categories and sections overlap with the service planning grid, there are unique elements to assess when rating support functions. A similar five-point rating scale may be developed for each of the categories in the following four sections.

Section 1: Client Satisfaction

Organizations have both internal and external clients. While it is common to think first of the external client—who seeks services from the organization's staff members—there is also an internal client, an employee of the organization who receives service from another employee of the organization. For example, a staff member who requests help developing a brochure is a client of the organization's communications or public relations department. This section assesses how well such a function serves its internal clients, the organization's staff members. Relationships with other staff members, timeliness in providing service, and communication skills are all aspects of internal client satisfaction.

Categories

Communication skills. To what degree do personnel working in administrative areas provide information and explanations that are clear and satisfactory to line staff members? A high rating might be given

Ratings: Five point scale where
5 = high
1 = low

Division / Service	Client satisfaction			Financial issues				Strategic placement			Impact of eliminating function		Total	Average
	Communication skills	Response time	Support/line function interrelationships	Other providers	Budget performance	Efficiency	Ability to compete on cost	Demand for support service	Innovation	Anticipation of future organization needs	Impact on support staff members	Other providers		

Figure 2. Planning Grid for Support Functions

to functions whose administrative staff members respond to inquiries and provide other information in a clearly communicated manner.

Response time. To what extent are support services provided in a timely fashion? Are staff members available when needed, and are deadlines met? A high rating could be given to functions that provide timely services and meet agreed-upon deadlines. Criteria for medium and low ratings could be set to reflect decreasing responsiveness and declining receipt of products by the agreed-upon deadline.

Support function/line function interrelationships. To what extent do staff members treat other staff members with courtesy and respect? High ratings might be given to functions with support staff who are always respectful and courteous to other staff members. Medium and low ratings could then be given in accord with diminished performance.

Section 2: Financial Issues

As in the evaluation of the line services, financial considerations are a frequent cause for concern, as income sources shrink and expenses grow. Because nonprofit organizations are mission driven, support functions are often one of the first areas examined when cost-saving measures are being planned. Comparisons can be based on what it would cost to have the function performed by an external contractor, the management's ability to control costs, and current staff member efficiency.

Categories

Other providers. Can these same functions be purchased from outside vendors or contractors? For example, can payroll be prepared by an outside organization? Can food service needs be met by an outside catering operation? A high rating might be given to support services that cannot readily be purchased from any external organization. A medium rating could be given to support services that could partially be provided by an external organization, although convenience and other factors might be negatively affected. A low rating may be given when functions can be contracted for readily, with little or no negative impact on the functioning of the organization.

Ability to compete on cost. What are the financial savings to the organization if an external contractor or vendor provides the same service? Depending on the function, guidelines can be developed to score a function as high, medium, or low in this category. For example, a high rating might be given to a function that is performed at a significantly lower cost to the organization than if it were to be performed by an external contractor or vendor. Significantly lower cost could be defined in terms of a dollar amount or a percentage in savings. Similarly, medium and low ratings might be given as external contractors become more and more competitively priced in relation to the cost of performing the same service internally.

A word of caution: Price is not the only criterion for determining whether a function could, or should, be performed by a contractor. Many an organization has found itself in trouble using outside vendors that did not have the capability to meet timelines or were not flexible enough to service the changing and complex needs of the nonprofit organization.

Budget performance. Has the function demonstrated its ability to control its financial performance over time, avoiding end-of-year budget deficits? Depending on what makes sense to the organization, a high rating might be given to functions that have operated within their allocated budgets for at least two consecutive years. A medium rating could be given to functions that occasionally had deficits, and a low rating to functions that continually fail to operate within their budgets.

Efficiency. To what extent could the function improve its ability to deliver the same products in a more cost-efficient manner? Could there be better work flows or ways to perform the function in fewer steps, with less red tape and fewer unnecessary procedures? A high rating might be given to a very efficient function, operating at its fullest capacity, while medium and low ratings could be given to functions of decreasing efficiency, with increasing room for improvement.

Section 3: Strategic Placement

This section of the grid rates the function's use of strategies that best serve the organization. Have employees been innovative, anticipating future needs as well as meeting current demands?

Categories

Demand for support services. As in the category described in section 4 of the planning grid for line functions, what has been the trend in requests for support services over the past few years? If the trend has been upward, a high rating could be given. A medium rating might be given to staff functions with a steady, but not decreasing number of requests for service, and a low rating to functions with declining requests for service.

Innovation. If an organization believes that innovation is important, then this value holds across both line and support functions. A high rating could be given to functions that have consistently tried to enhance services to line staff members in new and creative ways. Medium ratings might be given to functions that have made some modest attempts at innovation, and low ratings to services that have remained stagnant over the years.

Anticipating future needs of the organization. To what degree does the service address or anticipate future staff member or organizational needs? Are employees in support functions often taken by surprise, or can management be assured that the organization is in full compliance when changes are made in rules and regulations? Do employees in this function anticipate increased demands for support and make adjustments in preparation for this change? A high rating might be given to functions that are anticipatory in their thinking and actions, and are rarely taken by surprise or left unprepared. Medium and low ratings could be assigned to functions that are more focused on the present and less mindful of future changes that will directly impact the support services they offer.

Section 4: Impact of Eliminating Function

As in the line service planning grid, consideration of the effect on the organization of eliminating a support service is part of the downsizing process. Several of the categories overlap those in the service planning grid, and also include a rating on the necessity of the function. Caution must be exercised because support functions are so vital a part of the infrastructure of an organization. No organization, for example, can survive without a viable accounting capability. Institutions that license organizations or provide grants consider certain support functions fundamental to organizational competence. These considerations, however, cannot obviate the necessity to critically evaluate performance and to examine opportunities to perform these functions in more cost-efficient ways.

Impact on Support Staff Members

As with the planning grid for line functions, the degree to which support staff members would be affected if the service were contracted out or eliminated entirely may also be rated. Rating criteria can be developed based on the number of staff members in each support service and how feasible it would be to redirect them to other jobs within the organization. A high rating might be given to support services affecting a relatively high number of staff members, and medium to low ratings to support services affecting fewer staff members.

Impact on Other Providers

As described earlier, this category assesses whether the same support service could be purchased from outside vendors or contractors. A high rating might be given to support services that could not readily be purchased from any external organization. A medium rating might be given to support services that could partially be provided by an external organization, and a low rating might be given when support services could readily be contracted out with little or no negative impact on the functioning of the organization.

Other Uses for the Planning Grids

The planning grids may be used to assess the health of a particular service as well as to supply a profile of an entire division or organization. Managers using this tool will see obvious strengths to build upon and areas of weakness requiring improvement. Use of the grids over time may also result in the development of overall score or subscore ranges that signal good health or act as a warning for management. If there is little control over factors that lead to higher scores, reduction in discretionary funds, such as endowment support, for particular services should be considered. Any newly available discretionary funds may be used for a new venture that is part of the organization's strategic plan.

The Experience of the Village for Families and Children

As noted earlier, the authors used these planning grids during several budget processes. Top managers in each of the agency's six divisions completed the planning grids. The planning grid for line functions, in particular, has undergone extensive analysis and revision in an effort to develop category definitions that are as concise and concrete as possible, based on available objective information.

Despite these efforts, several difficulties were discovered. When each of the top managers assessed the services in his or her division, a rating style factor emerged that influenced category judgments. Some raters tended to be conservative and others were more liberal.

There are several ways to deal with rater style differences. One is to compare rankings of services made by a particular rater. Thus, services are comparatively high or low within a rater's division. Tempering rating styles by having more than one rater evaluate a particular service is another way. Cross-ratings can be made by various members of the top management group, or by both the service's director and the division's top manager, or by the organization's president and the division's top manager. A third strategy relates to the original goal of developing concrete categories not open to interpretation, such as current level of endowment support and proportion of urban/low income clients. Wherever possible, a staff member from management information services or bookkeeping should complete some of the category ratings.

In summary, the downsizing experience encourages organizations to examine the alignment of services and products with its mission and strategic priorities. Downsizing also helps nonprofit organizations plan for future events that may adversely affect them. Finally, downsizing forces a critical examination of each and every part of the organization, whether it be a line or a support function, and identifies ways in which each service and the organization as a whole may be strengthened. It is equally important to have a systematic approach to decision-making that is readily communicated to, and understood by, all the key constituents in and around the nonprofit organization.

9

Adapting These Models to the Small Organization

The models described in this book were developed by the authors in an organization of approximately 160 staff members. The principles underlying the models, however, are applicable to nonprofit organizations regardless of size. This chapter suggests ways in which the models may be adapted to smaller organizations.

Governance and Board Development

Regardless of size, nonprofit organizations have governing bodies, usually boards of directors, that are responsible for such activities as setting policy, approving budgets, and hiring the top executive. The boards often function from year to year without a critical examination of structures and roles that may require modification as conditions change. Periodic self-examination is essential for every board, although the process may be less formal for a small board. Instead of commissioning a task force to investigate the current governance, all members of a small board may participate in the assessment. [See ed. note]

As a group, the board members can question whether the existing written governance follows current practice. Is there any indication that the governance is no longer appropriate, such as a major crisis? Other signals that all is not well include poor attendance at board meetings and time spent on unimportant agenda items and trivial decisions.

It is critical that the board of directors involve the organization's top executive in discussing any problems in the functioning of the board and its present governance. Identifying these problems will result in objectives for a new governance.

111

Periodic review of board members' responsibilities is helpful for organizations of any size. New board members may be unclear about their roles even after a formal orientation if they have to digest a lot of information. Board members who have been acting in that capacity for a long time may find this periodic review a helpful update on some responsibilities. Because every board has a limited number of places, its effectiveness depends on careful selection of members and continual review and strengthening of this process.

Follow-up assessment of a new governance is an important step, regardless of the organization's size. It might be as simple as scheduling a meeting of the full board and top executive a year after significant changes are made to see whether they had the desired impact. Sometimes changes to correct one deficit lead to new problems, and these have to be identified as well. A small organization that has a staff member responsible for planning, evaluation, or quality assurance would find it helpful to ask her or him to lead the board and the top executive in an objective review.

Developing the Leadership Team

It is conceivable that a very small organization might consist of an executive director, clinical staff members, and volunteers, and there would not be a leadership team. For slightly larger organizations, however, with perhaps an executive and two program directors, the discussion in chapter 2 may be relevant, if *leadership team* is interpreted broadly to include such a configuration. The actual name of the team—perhaps Management Team or Futures Committee—is less important than the fact of its existence. It should be a name that is comfortable for the executive director.

The advantage of a group or team as compared to an individual is the diversity of opinions and approaches that can be brought to decision-making. Another advantage to forming such a team, in the small organization, is the cohesiveness and team effort that develop when all are involved in decision-making, and the greater likelihood of buy-in when decisions have been reached.

The considerations in selecting and commissioning the team that were outlined for the large organization in chapter 2 apply to the small organization as well. For example, the top executive, if given a choice, should select members whose problem-solving styles, skills, and experience complement one another's. The top executive should set the tone for team members to participate freely and equally in discussion and decision-making, regardless of their position in the organization. It is also important for the top executive to identify at the outset whether the final decision regarding any particular task rests with the executive director or the full leadership group. The best outcome is an increasingly stronger voice for the leadership group as trust develops.

The management is expected to develop a vision that will guide the organization into the future as it strives to fulfill its mission. The steps outlined in chapter 2 apply to the leadership team regardless of the size of the organization. If there are few managers to share responsibility, it behooves the team to place particular importance on establishing priorities for the strategic objectives, as only those very high on the list may be tackled in the near future.

Regular performance assessment is necessary to the evolving effectiveness of any team, and is especially critical for the newly formed team. Areas where bumps or difficulties arose during the past year or months should be discussed candidly, along with possible strategies to overcome these barriers. Patience and a willingness to share responsibilities will go a long way toward developing a thriving and effective team.

Strategic Planning

Changes in funding, social trends, and population shifts are affecting all nonprofit organizations. Strategic planning is particularly important to small organizations because they are relatively fragile, having fewer income-generating options than large organizations. Strategic planning encourages decision-making based on assessment of the current environment and what it means to the future of the organization. The process also encourages a thorough assessment of strengths and weaknesses, ability and willingness to take risks, as well as systematic feedback on the accomplishment of plans.

The key components of strategic planning, as outlined in chapter 3, also pertain to the small organization. A SWOT analysis (Strengths, Weaknesses, Opportunities, and Threats), for example, should be performed for all the agency's services, regardless of how many or how few there are.

The situational assessment, which is the first part of the SWOT analysis, may be modified or streamlined for an organization that has few individual services to examine. Rather than an elaborate situational self-assessment survey, the single-service or small organization may be able to do this evaluation in structured group meetings. Focus groups can concentrate on responding to specific questions about the strengths and weaknesses of services. It would be advisable, however, to write up the results of the group meeting as documentation, to be referred back to during the strategic planning process and during presentations to the board of directors and other audiences.

The environmental scan, which is the second part of the SWOT analysis, is time-consuming but indispensable, regardless of an organization's size. It may not be necessary for the small organization to carry out its own environmental scan. Other organizations may have already identified future trends that could be opportunities or threats to the organization. Environmental scans produced by major national organizations such as the United Way and Family Service America are often available to member agencies.

Focus groups of community leaders can provide relatively inexpensive information on local trends. The organization may broaden its community support and financial opportunities as a result of this contact with the community's leaders. College students interested in a field placement may also prove invaluable in gathering information at minimal cost to the nonprofit organization.

The identification of strategic priorities is critical to strategic planning. A group can be formed to participate in this process. If the organization has fewer than 10 employees, it is quite possible to involve all staff members in the identification process. Internal and external feasibility studies on the reduced list of trends, problems, and issues should still take place.

A strategic action plan should be developed regardless of the organization's size. For the small organization, it is easy to involve all staff members in brainstorming ideas for possible new services or products germane to the strategic priorities. When staff members have been part of the development of the strategic action plan, they feel ownership and commitment to realizing the goals it outlines. For staff members to participate successfully, however, they must fully understand the role of the board of directors in decision-making.

As has been emphasized throughout this book, monitoring is a critical step in assessing progress and change. This is true for any strategic plan in any size organization, because without monitoring, the strategic plan may be just a theoretical exercise that is never carried out. Although the small organization is unlikely to have a research or evaluation department, an individual or a small group can be assigned the task of coordinating and leading this assessment. Self-monitoring can work especially well if participants are open and feel comfortable discussing any roadblocks that might keep them from accomplishing the strategic plan.

Outcome Effectiveness Studies

Because of the requirements of outside funders, many nonprofit organizations, regardless of size, are being asked to measure their effectiveness. For this reason, among others, these studies are not optional. The question is not whether, but how to conduct such a study, given limited resources and perhaps limited experience in this activity.

Many of the ideas in chapter 4 can be adapted to the small organization. For example, the multiple measures approach may be carried out with the help of college students or volunteers in collecting information. Because of the confidential nature of the study, however, it is important to identify a single individual who will maintain the collected information confidentially and present a summary of the findings.

Ideally, a researcher, evaluator, quality-assurance manager, planner, or some other individual on staff has the capability to coordinate such a study. An alternative is to collaborate or contract with another nonprofit organization that does have such expertise. A local college or university may also be able to take on some of these activities on a pro bono basis.

It is important that the organization not equate a client satisfaction survey with an outcome effectiveness study. For all the reasons set forth in chapter 4, this is clearly not acceptable. In fact, it will be difficult to make such an error if time is spent developing a clear and accurate definition of service effectiveness. Demonstrated and documented service effectiveness is at the heart of every social service organization, and is important not only to funders but to the organization as a whole.

Organizational Health

The health of an organization directly affects the quality of its services. If that quality is low, and other providers are available, the viability of the organization is threatened. Particularly for the organization that may have a small client or customer base, loss of even one major client can have dramatic consequences.

Services of the highest quality can be delivered only when employee morale is high and service providers feel valued, enthusiastic about their work, and committed to the organization. The model outlined in chapter 5 may be used to assess the small organization's healthy functioning. A group of concerned managers, for example, can first identify questions they would like answered about the health of the organization. The chapter provides a guide for possible items to include in a survey of organizational well-being.

Through professional networks and conferences, it is often possible to borrow a survey, perhaps of the type referred to as an employee-satisfaction survey, from a similar organization, and adapt it to fit one's own. Using a survey rather than, say, a focus group format has the advantage that staff members may be more candid in their responses if they feel that confidentiality is safeguarded and that findings will be presented without identification.

Another alternative is to have the staff member responsible for human resources or personnel conduct individual interviews with employees. He or she can then summarize the findings in confidentiality. This option will be viable, however, only if that individual is not the top executive and is trusted by his or her colleagues.

A note of caution: A study should never be undertaken for show. It is acceptable to study organizational health only if top management is committed to acting on the findings. If that commitment is absent, the process can be destructive for staff members, whose expectations for change have been raised, and the entire organization can be destabilized.

Awareness and Image

The community's awareness and perceptions of an organization influence its ability to deliver services to those in need. Before any particular service can be sought, community residents must know of its existence and have certain information about the organization. Who may receive services from this organization? How much does it charge? Is it affiliated with a state agency, a religious organization, or some other group?

It is worthwhile for a small organization to invest time and effort in researching the community's awareness and perceptions, so that misperceptions can be arrested and information supplied. A small organization with limited resources may tackle this undertaking with the help of internship students from the local college or university, or perhaps a retired executive or other person willing to do pro bono or volunteer work.

In any event, it is helpful to periodically canvas community leaders, residents, and potential sources of referrals, such as other nonprofit organizations, to test the current level of awareness and the effect of the organization's efforts. The information gathered may be useful in planning ways to attract charitable contributions. Learning what are the most salient characteristics of the organization also helps in developing and publicizing services.

Downsizing

All nonprofit organizations have struggled financially during the recent hard times. The small nonprofit may be particularly vulnerable to shifts in funding, and have no choice but to reduce expenses if it is to remain viable.

The tools presented in chapter 8, while used by the authors in a large organization, may still apply to the smaller organization. Being proactive and anticipatory is always vital. Contingency plans are necessary in case funding shortfalls occur. In a volatile funding environment, all organizations, regardless of size, should have a plan, particularly in those spheres of work where income sources are in greatest jeopardy. This plan should identify specific revenue enhancements or expense reductions based on trend analyses and cash-flow projections.

In the small organization, where there may not be a leadership team, it is especially important to involve staff members in the budgeting process. At a minimum, they should be kept informed of developments and solicited for ways to handle shortfalls; at a maximum, they should present proposals and suggestions to the top executive and participate in the difficult decisions that may have to be made.

Further, if the categories in the chapter 8 planning grids are pertinent to an organization, only modest alterations may be needed to use them. These grids offer a framework for involving staff members in examining issues in an objective, rather than an emotional, manner.

The concepts discussed in this book should be of interest to the nonprofit organization whatever its size. Changing times require nothing less than excellence in the struggle to survive and flourish.

Job Descriptions for Officers of the Agency

Chair of the Board: Position Description

Job Summary

1. Assures that the board of directors develops and monitors strategic objectives and policies, and fulfills its responsibilities for the governance of the agency.

2. Consults with the president to help him or her achieve the mission of the agency.

3. Optimizes the relationship between the board and management.

4. Consults with and advises the president in the execution of operational responsibilities.

Responsibilities and Duties

1. Presides over meetings and provides leadership to ensure that the board and its executive committee function effectively, interact with management optimally, and fulfill all required duties.

2. Develops agendas in consultation with the president and the board officers.

3. Recommends, in consultation with the president and the board officers, the composition of the board committees.

4. Assists the president and the nominating committee in recruiting board members and others for whatever volunteer assignments are needed.

5. Reflects any concerns management has in regard to the role of the board of directors or individual directors. Reflects to the president the concerns of the board of directors and other constituencies.

119

6. Presents to the board an evaluation of the pace, direction, and organizational strength of the agency.

7. Prepares and conducts reviews of the president's performance, in consultation with the executive committee, and submits a proposed compensation package to the compensation committee.

8. Focuses the board's attention on matters of agency governance that relate to its own structure, role, and relationship to management. Assures that the board is satisfied it has fulfilled all of its responsibilities.

9. Acts as an additional set of eyes and ears for the chief executive officer.

10. Proposes candidates to the nominating committee for nomination at the annual meeting of the corporation, thus assuring orderly succession in board leadership.

11. Acts as principal board policy spokesperson both internally and externally.

12. Appoints ad hoc task forces as conditions require.

13. Represents the board of directors at key community meetings.

14. Plans the annual meeting for the corporation.

15. Stands as an ex-officio member, with voice and vote, on all standing committees.

16. Recommends ways to assure continuing familiarity and connectedness of board members with the agency.

Vice Chair of the Board: Position Description

Job Summary

1. Discharges the duties of the chair of the board in his or her absence.

2. Provides leadership to the standing committee to which he or she is elected.

3. Serves on the agency's executive committee.

Responsibilities and Duties

1. Plans and carries out committee objectives and responsibilities.

2. Develops effective and efficient board participation in committee functions.

3. Reports to the executive committee and board of directors on the work of the committee.

4. Advises the chief executive officer of the committee's agenda, and requests any management support required.

5. Assists the chair of the board in appraising the performance of the president.

6. Monitors and evaluates progress on the board's strategic objectives and related service delivery.

7. Gives leadership, as circumstances warrant, to the role and functions of the committee he or she chairs.

8. Assists the chair of the board in assuring effective delineation between the board's responsibilities and management's responsibilities.

Secretary of the Board: Position Description

Job Summary

The secretary assumes responsibilities as corporate secretary as defined by state law and required in authorization of service contracts with, for example, the state's department of children and youth services.

Responsibilities and Duties

1. Edits and/or records minutes of the meetings of the board of directors and executive committee.

2. Knows the content and location of official agency documents.

3. Verifies the management's authority to authorize contracts.

4. Acts as board correspondent or in similar capacities as directed by the chair of the board.

5. Recommends policies for retaining agency historical records, and ensures their preservation.

Treasurer of the Board: Position Description

Job Summary

The treasurer assumes lead responsibility within the capital stewardship committee for monitoring and periodically reporting the agency's financial condition.

Responsibilities and Duties

1. Periodically reviews the agency's financial records and reports to the executive committee and to the board of directors on the agency's financial condition.

2. Assures that reporting is correct, financial records are up to date, and retention and disposal standards are met.

3. Collaborates with management on financial matters and trends.

4. Collaborates with management on budget planning and on forecasting endowment income.

5. Serves as a member of the capital stewardship committee.

Assistant Treasurer: Position Description

Job Summary

Assumes the lead responsibility with the capital stewardship committee for communications with independent auditors, and assumes the responsibilities of the treasurer in his or her absence.

Responsibilities and Duties

1. Periodically evaluates the performance of auditors and issues requests for proposals as circumstances warrant.

2. Makes periodic reports to the executive committee and board of directors on the agency's financial status, in the absence of the treasurer and in accordance with the treasurer's duties and responsibilities.

3. Reports the outcome of the independent audit to the board of directors.

4. Serves on the capital stewardship committee.

Chief Executive Officer: Position Description

Job Summary

1. Serves as chief operating officer of the organization, accepting responsibility for operational success or failure.

2. With the chair of the board, enables the board of directors to fulfill its governance function, and facilitates optimum interaction between management and the board of directors.

3. Gives direction to the formulation of and leadership to the achievement of the organization's philosophy, mission, and strategy, and to its annual objectives and goals.

Responsibilities and Duties

To the Board of Directors

1. With the chair of the board, develops agendas for meetings, so

that the board can fulfill all its responsibilities effectively. Develops an annual calendar to cover all crucial issues in a timely fashion.

2. Ensures that the board and its chair are kept fully informed on the condition of the organization and on all important factors influencing it.

3. Secures the best thinking and involvement of each board member.

4. Works with the chair to make the committee structure of the board function effectively.

5. With the chair, recommends the composition of the board and its committees.

6. Identifies areas calling for board policy development and guides policy development.

To Operations

1. Assures that the organization's philosophy and mission statements are pertinent and practiced throughout the agency.

2. Assures that the organization has a long-range plan to achieve its mission, toward which it makes consistent and timely progress.

3. Assures that the flow of funds permits the organization to make steady progress toward the achievement of its mission, and that those funds are allocated properly to reflect present needs and future potential.

4. Develops an effective management team with provision for succession.

5. Ensures the development and implementation of personnel training and development plans and programs to provide the human resources necessary for the achievement of the organization's mission.

6. Maintains a climate that attracts, keeps, and motivates top quality people, both professional and volunteer.

7. Formulates and assures consistent administration of major operational and procedural policies.

8. Serves as the chief executive spokesperson for the organization, thereby assuring needed representation with the organization's various constituents.

9. Develops and maintains community networks crucial to the operation and function of the organization and to the development of needed human services.

J ob Descriptions for Board Committees

Executive Committee

An executive committee shall be elected by the board of directors. Its membership will include the officers and up to three at-large members as conditions or needs require. The chair of the board will chair the executive committee.

The executive committee shall, when the board of directors is not in session, have all the authority of the board of directors except in the following matters: (1) the filling of vacancies on the board of directors, (2) the election of officers, (3) the appointment of standing committees, (4) the adoption of agency strategic objectives, and (5) the adoption of the annual budget.

The executive committee shall, in consultation with the president, prepare the annual budget plan for presentation to, and adoption by, the board. The executive committee shall have full authority to revise the current annual budget plan as conditions warrant, but not to exceed a 10% modification.

The executive committee shall receive and review all board committee or task force reports and shall prepare recommendations to the board for appropriate decision and action.

Strategic Planning and Evaluation Committee

The strategic planning and evaluation committee shall be responsible for

1. Periodically reviewing, and making recommendations for, agency strategic objectives;

125

2. Annually evaluating and reporting on the attainment of strategic objectives;

3. Planning and conducting periodic community forums in conjunction with the public issues committee.

4. Advising the executive committee on policies needing amendment or development to enable the agency to carry its mission and strategic objectives forward.

Members of this committee shall be elected at the annual meeting of the corporation.

Financial Resource Development Committee

The financial resource development committee shall be responsible for

1. Developing a direct and deferred giving program and managing capital campaigns when required;

2. Coordinating with, and giving support to, allied constituents who manage fundraisers;

3. Developing appreciation events as required.

Members of this committee shall be elected at the annual meeting of the corporation.

Public Issues Committee

The public issues committee shall be responsible for

1. Monitoring municipal, state, and federal legislative and administrative activities affecting the delivery of services to, and the well-being of, children, adults, families, and nonprofit voluntary agencies;

2. Preparing policy positions for recommendation to the executive committee and board of directors;

3. Sponsoring and participating in an annual meeting with legislators to acquaint them with key issues affecting families and the agency; and

4. Establishing procedures for providing agency testimony on important municipal, state, and federal issues.

Members of this committee shall be elected at the annual meeting of the corporation.

Capital Stewardship Committee

The capital stewardship committee shall be responsible for

1. Formulating capital investment policies and management objectives governing buying, selling, exchanging, and transferring stocks, bonds, securities, and real estate;

2. Selecting one or more investment managers and delegating to one or more investment managers such investment responsibilities as it deems prudent;

3. Authorizing and empowering the treasurer to execute, on behalf of the corporation, such documents as may be necessary to effect the purchase, sale, exchange, and transfer of securities or real estate;

4. Setting policies and management objectives to govern the use, care, and development of real estate owned by the corporation;

5. Engaging independent auditors who shall annually evaluate the Corporation's fiscal performance and management conformity with standards of accounting for nonprofit organizations; and

6. Reporting the findings of the independent audit to the board of directors in each annual meeting of the corporation.

Members of this committee shall be elected at the annual meeting of the corporation.

Nominating Committee

The nominating committee shall be responsible for

1. Evaluating board and committee membership needs, in consultation with the chair of the board and the president and vice chair of the committee;

2. Monitoring the attendance and performance of board members;

3. Recruiting and selecting nominees for board membership; and

4. Orienting new board members and supporting existing board members as needed.

The nominating committee shall receive committee membership recommendations from the chair of the board, in consultation with the president and vice chair of this committee, at the annual meeting of the corporation.

Members of this committee shall be elected at the annual meeting of the corporation.

Compensation Committee

The compensation committee shall be responsible for

1. Reviewing compensation packages for top managers of the agency, and
2. Voting on top management's compensation packages.

The compensation package for the president shall be recommended to the committee by the chair of the board. The compensation package(s) for other top management personnel shall be recommended to the committee by the president of the corporation.

The chair of the board shall appoint members to the compensation committee.

Ad Hoc Task Forces

In the course of fulfilling board responsibilities, it is likely that special issues or tasks may arise requiring the formation of ad hoc task forces to evaluate and frame recommendations to either the executive committee or the board of directors.

In such events, the chair of the board will appoint necessary task forces to consider specific issues on a time-limited basis.

Such issues might be

- Major benefit programs, such as the pension program
- Compensation for top management
- Special issues raised by major funders
- Major human resources issues
- Major planning regarding agency property development

Answers to Questions about the New Agency Governance

How Do We Distinguish Board Policy from Operational Policy?

Matters over which the board has responsibility are largely defined in committee job descriptions. Matters pertaining to the daily functioning of the agency and related policies and procedures are considered operational issues. When a particular matter requires delineation between board roles and responsibilities and management roles and responsibilities, it is the responsibility of the chair of the board and the president to bring that matter forward to the executive committee.

How Were These Particular Committees Selected?

The recommended committees are those most closely aligned with policy matters within the area of the board's responsibility. The provision for ad hoc task forces affords the chair of the board the flexibility to engage the board on other matters and at the same time use board members' time and talents most efficiently.

Under the proposed new structure, the program and planning committee and the strategic planning task force are replaced by the strategic planning and evaluation committee. The functions of the board human resources committee and the facilities and administration committee are considered a responsibility of top management because they are closely tied to agency operations. In addition, a task force could be appointed to study problems identified in the application of any policy.

The board of directors will periodically offer community focus groups for key community representatives. In these forums, agency plans and achievements will be reviewed and participants will be asked to develop a community issues and needs statement to assist the organization in its strategic planning. Staff support will be given by the research department and the communication and development department.

In addition, management will implement plans for periodic consumer focus groups to assess the agency's services structure. The objective will be to create greater connectedness with consumers and improve understanding of service delivery effectiveness.

How Will These Proposals Be Implemented?

The strategic planning task force understands that implementation of these proposals needs to be managed carefully. While size can and will be managed by attrition and rotation, the board may simultaneously need to elect new members to achieve the desired mix of skills and representation.

The strategic planning task force recommends that a period of three years be allocated for the process, and that any revised bylaws include the needed transitional plan and language.

Conversion to the new structure requires legal review and bylaw revision prior to implementation. When the board adopts new bylaws, the committee structure will change.

Is the Authority Vested in the President Appropriate?

If the board is accountable for the well-being of the agency, then it must be able to hold top management clearly responsible and accountable for the adequacy of the agency's operations. The board's responsibility for evaluation and control may in fact be strengthened by this plan, as the board will have a basis on which to appraise the president's performance.

How Will We Know if the Plan Is Successful?

There should be a rather quick reduction in board member frustration as a consequence of greater clarity and focus in meetings. However, it will take some months for the entire board to become comfortable with changes at the policy level.

How Will Board Members Network with Agency Services?

Board members must clearly understand the services that fulfill the agency's mission. The reduced demand for board member time in meetings will permit the development of greater opportunities to learn about service issues and successes. Further, board members' interest in the agency should increase with the alleviation of former frustrations. Through this new clarification of roles and responsibilities, carried out in a timely manner, board, management and staff will better meet the needs of our children and families.

About the Authors

Miriam P. Kluger, who holds a Ph.D. in applied psychological research and evaluation from Hofstra University, Hempstead, NY, is senior vice president for research and planning at the Village for Families and Children, Inc., Hartford, CT. Before joining the Village staff she was a health care analyst at Queens Hospital Community Mental Health Center in Jamaica, NY, and a staff manager in public relations for A T & T Communications, Bedminster, NJ. She is a member of the National Council on Research in Child Welfare and is listed in the 1990 Who's Who, *Women in American Business.*

William A. Baker is president of the Village for Families and Children, Inc., Hartford, CT, and former executive director of the Family and Children's Service Society of Summit County, Akron, OH. Baker earned his M.S.W. at the University of Michigan, Ann Arbor, MI. A member of the CWLA National Advisory Council and the steering committee for the CWLA North Atlantic Region, he also sits on the board of Family Service America, chairs the United Way Executive's Forum, and serves on the Connecticut Governor's Task Force on Adoption.